P9-CRA-304

Thinking Like a Teacher

Using Observational Assessment to Improve Teaching and Learning

Samuel J. Meisels
Erikson Institute

Helen L. Harrington
University of Michigan

with

Patricia McMahon
American Institutes for Research

Margo L. Dichtelmiller
Eastern Michigan University

Judy R. Jablon
Rebus Inc

Allyn and Bacon
Boston ■ London ■ Toronto ■ Sydney ■ Tokyo ■ Singapore

WITHDRAWN FROM
J. EUGENE SMITH LIBRARY
EASTERN CONN. STATE UNIVERSITY
WILLIMANTIC, CT. 06226-2295

Series Editor: Arnis E. Burvikovs
Editorial Assistant: Matthew Forster
Marketing Manager: Kathleen Morgan
Production Editor: Michael Granger
Editorial Production Service: Modern Graphics, Inc.
Composition Buyer: Linda Cox
Manufacturing Buyer: Julie McNeill
Cover Administrator: Kristina Mose-Libon
Electronic Composition: Modern Graphics, Inc.

Copyright © 2002 by Allyn & Bacon
A Pearson Education Company
75 Arlington Street
Boston, MA 02116

Internet: www.ablongman.com

All rights reserved. No part of the material protected by this copyright notice may be reproduced or uti-
lized in any form or by any means, electronic or mechanical, including photocopying, recording, or by
any information storage and retrieval system, without written permission from the copyright owner.

Between the time Website information is gathered and then published, it is not unusual for some sites
to have closed. Also, the transcription of URLs can result in unintended typographical errors. The publisher would appreciate notification where these occur so that they may be corrected in subsequent
editions.

Library of Congress Cataloging-in-Publication Data

Meisels, Samuel J.
    Thinking like a teacher : using observational assessment to improve teaching and
learning   / Samuel J. Meisels, Helen L. Harrington with Patricia McMahon, Margo L.
Dichtelmiller, Judy R. Jablon.
        p. cm.
    Includes bibliographical references.
    ISBN 0-205-33175-0 (alk. paper)
     1. Observation (Educational method) 2. Early childhood education--Evaluation. I.
Harrington, Helen L. II. Title.

LB1027.28 .M45 2001
372.13--dc21   2001031803

Printed in the United States of America

10 9 8 7 6 5 4 3 2 1   05 04 03 02 01

Contents

Chapter 4   **Assessing Learning   98**

Appendixes

Preface

This book focuses on helping prospective teachers begin to think like a teacher. The process of pedagogical knowledge that this requires calls for an understanding of the reasons for doing particular things in classrooms and learning about the importance of accumulating evidence to justify instructional decisions and plans.

The book is also dedicated to helping prospective teachers make connections between teaching, learning, and assessment. In particular, we pay close attention to the use of assessment information in the process of planning and instruction by focusing on the Work Sampling System, an observational assessment that uses the framework of an authentic performance assessment to teach new teachers about observing, recording, and evaluating student activity.

This book contains more than forty hands-on assignments and task sheets that are designed to provide practice in:

- observing, documenting, and assessing learning,
- guiding children in self-assessment,
- connecting theory to practice,
- beginning to see the relationship between child development knowledge and curriculum and instruction,
- designing individualized goals and instruction, and
- learning how to plan activities grounded in knowledge of students and curricular goals.

Overall, the book is intended to help prospective teachers gain a sense of what to teach, what to look for while observing students, what to document about children's learning, and how to assess the impact of one's own personal performance and achievements. These goals are accomplished through a variety of hands-on assignments in and out of class and in the field and are accompanied by use of the Work Sampling *Omnibus Guidelines* that provide detailed information about instructional standards and objectives for children from preschool to grade 5. We are confident that this book and the *Guidelines* will not only help prospective teachers begin to think like a teacher, but will provide a basis for continuing professional development.

This book was first published in a different format by Rebus Inc, the publisher of the Work Sampling System. Called *Observing, Documenting, and Assessing: The Work Sampling System Handbook for Teacher Educators,* it focused on presenting the ideas incorporated in this book to those who prepare prospective teachers. The present version of this text has been rewritten from the student's—or prospective teacher's—point of view. It is accompanied by an Instructor's Manual that is published separately.

Samuel J. Meisels
Helen Harrington
Pat McMahon
Margo Dichtelmiller
Judy Jablon

Acknowledgments

Several colleagues made invaluable contributions to the development of the original Handbook. Carolyn Burns assisted us in numerous ways, especially in reworking the student assignments. The other authors of the Work Sampling System, Dot Marsden and Aviva Dorfman, were a constant source of ideas and support. Paula Bousley and Patty Humphrey did a wonderful and tireless job of preparing the manuscript, and Frank deSanto was our copyeditor for the first edition.

In addition, we were the fortunate recipients of advice and recommendations from a distinguished Advisory Council of teacher educators and practitioners. We are very grateful to Lauren Ashley, Academy School, Brattleboro, VT; Terry Berkeley, Towson State University, Towson, MD; Joni Block, Wheelock College, Boston, MA; Timothy Boerst, South Redford Public Schools, Redford, MI; Amy Colton, National Board for Professional Teaching Standards; Cynthia Dieterich, Cleveland State University, Cleveland, OH; Aviva Dorfman, University of Michigan, Ann Arbor, MI; Ellen Frede, Trenton State College, Trenton, NJ; Patty Horsch, Erikson Institute, Chicago, IL; Sylvia Jones, Eastern Michigan University, Ypsilanti, MI; Nancy Klein, Cleveland State University, Cleveland, OH; Therese M. Kuhs, University of South Carolina, Columbia, SC; Kathy Lake, Alverno College, Milwaukee, WI; Joan G. Leonard, Hollis Elementary School, Hollis, NH; Christine B. Maxwell, University of Wisconsin-Milwaukee, Milwaukee, WI; Carlota Schechter, Central Connecticut State University, West Hartford, CT; Claudia Schuster, Central Connecticut State University, New Britain, CT; and Dinah Volk, Cleveland State University, Cleveland, OH. Finally, we also want to acknowledge the support of the University of Michigan School of Education where this work had its inception.

None of this would have been possible without the support of the Joyce Foundation. Although the opinions expressed are solely those of the authors, we are very grateful to the Foundation and in particular, to Peter Mich, for enabling this work to come to fruition.

Samuel J. Meisels
Helen Harrington
Pat McMahon
Margo Dichtelmiller
Judy Jablon

CHAPTER 1

The Work Sampling System and Teacher Preparation

Learning to teach is very complex. One the most difficult and important tasks you will encounter as a student of teaching is learning how to make thoughtful, reasoned decisions as an ongoing part of your professional practice. This book is designed to aid in that endeavor. It was prompted by our work with preservice teachers and by our desire to incorporate into teacher preparation some of the insights we have acquired from teaching others to use the Work Sampling System, a comprehensive curriculum-embedded performance assessment. We have used this performance assessment with early childhood and elementary teacher preparation students and have found it to be a powerful tool that encourages them to begin to "think like teachers." We hope you will find it valuable as well.

In this chapter we discuss the particular model of teacher preparation that the book is intended to support, a model grounded in teachers' understanding of the role of assessment in teaching and learning. We will briefly introduce the Work Sampling System and discuss its relevance to new forms of performance assessment, pointing out how you can use it to help you develop a rich sense of the connections among teaching, learning, and assessment. We will also present an overview of this book and discuss how you can get the most out of it.

A. Model of Teacher Preparation

This book supports a model of teacher preparation that views teaching and learning as complex, interactive processes. The experiences children bring with them, the activities they engage in while in classrooms, and the curriculum materials they interact with all serve to ground and direct their learning. In this model of teaching, learning is viewed as a constructive process that occurs for individuals within social contexts. Teachers play a key role in helping children construct knowledge in meaningful ways within the school context. This model goes beyond a child-centered approach, however, to one that views teachers and learners as co-constructors of knowledge. Just as children bring their own understanding to the learning they engage in within the classroom, so too do teachers. Teachers' ability to foster meaningful learning in children is influenced by the materials they use, the tasks they design, the contexts they establish within the classroom, and their own understanding of each child as a learner. Each of these factors is influenced, in turn, by how teachers perceive their roles and responsibilities for fostering children's learning and development.

Assumptions of this model of teacher preparation include the beliefs that fostering meaningful learning is a key responsibility of all teachers; that student learning encompasses social, personal, and physical development as well as cognitive development; that cognitive development occurs across all aspects of the typical elementary curriculum; and that meaningful learning is an overall goal for all children. Teachers fulfill these responsibilities by first coming to know each child as a learner. This is accomplished through systematic and ongoing observation, through thoughtful and rigorous documentation of meaningful learning, and through the continuous assessment of the achievements and the learning opportunities provided for children. The interaction among children's learning, the classroom opportunities provided for them, and the teacher's modification of those opportunities is directed by both teachers and children and is an ongoing part of classroom life. This model of teaching assumes that assessment, both formal and informal, is fundamental to teaching. But we wish to emphasize a different approach to assessment than has traditionally been taught in teacher preparation programs. Ours is an approach to assessment that views teaching as a complex, ambiguous task for which there are few absolute answers. In this view of teaching, one of the goals of teacher education programs is to prepare prospective teachers for this complexity. This is done by helping them develop the skills to find their own answers to the teaching dilemmas embedded in practice, and by fostering the ability to determine the best answers from among a range of possible solutions. A key assumption is that an understanding of new approaches to assessment is essential to responsible and effective teaching.

B. Teaching and Assessment

For decades, assessment in American schools has been dominated by group-administered, norm-referenced, multiple-choice achievement tests. These tests often hold the power to change how teachers and children view themselves and their role in the educational process. But recent research and practice have shown that these tests may do more harm than good. They narrow the curriculum. They reduce children's motivation to learn. They stigmatize low-achieving learners. They give families very little information about their children's accomplishments. And they shift the focus of the educational process from what is taught in classrooms to an examination of the data that can be used for accountability (Calfee, 1987; Darling-Hammond & Wise, 1985; Fredriksen, 1984; Fredriksen & Collins, 1989; Haladyna, Nolen, & Haas, 1991; Haney, 1991; Koretz, 1988; Linn, 1987; Mehrens, 1992; Mehrens & Kaminsky, 1989; Meisels, 1989, 1994; Neill & Medina, 1991; Shepard, 1989).

These approaches to assessment ignore the ambiguously structured nature of the teaching and learning process. They fail to acknowledge that there are few single "correct" answers to most of the dilemmas encountered in teaching; what works for one student may not work for others, an effective pedagogical approach in one domain may be ineffective in another, and how one child demonstrates understanding may bear little relationship to how another child demonstrates understanding in the same area of learning.

Although these problems have been detected at all levels K–12, they are of particular concern at the start of schooling, when children are first exposed to formal instruction and are beginning to make the transition from child-centered preschool and kindergarten programs. Group-administered achievement tests are of little practical value for learning about the academic achievement of these children. These types of tests are based upon a set of specific psychometric assumptions about the measurement of learning that are not highly relevant to young children (Meisels, 1994, 2000) or to how we currently understand learning (Bransford, Brown, & Cocking, 1999; Shepard, 2000). The emphasis on reliability of scoring and measurement in these tests focuses on learning that can be quantified and measured accurately. This focus is consistent with a model of teaching and learning in which teaching consists of the transmission of knowledge to students, and learning consists of the students' acquisition of skills and facts. The tests do not measure such important understandings as students' ability to engage in critical thinking; to analyze, synthesize, and draw conclusions; or to apply their skills and conceptual knowledge when solving problems. For young children just entering school, repeated exposure to this style of teaching and learning may establish long-lasting negative expectations about what learning consists of, how students should respond to new information, and how far to exercise intellectual initiative and curiosity (Paris, Lawton, Turner, & Roth, 1991; Urdan & Paris, 1994).

C. *Performance Assessment*

Performance assessments were developed in order to change the focus of instruction and to improve teaching and outcomes for students. These assessments are based on a new understanding of how to measure educational achievement and they assume a different approach to teaching and learning from conventional models of simple transmission of information from teachers to students (Calfee, 1987, 1992; Fredriksen, 1984; Linn, 2000; Shavelson, Baxter, & Pine, 1992; Stiggins, 1991; Stiggins, Conklin, & Bridgeford, 1986; Wolf, Bixby, Glenn, & Gardner, 1991; Wolf, LeMahieu, & Eresh, 1992). In this model, teaching is seen as an activity in which teachers facilitate the process of students' learning, and learning is conceptualized as the students' construction of knowledge through active engagement with their world. In order to create assessments that are relevant to this kind of instruction, the content and structure of assessment must change.

Rather than asking students to respond to multiple choice items, the new assessments are performance-based and rely upon extended opportunities for student engagement in complex tasks (Shepard, 1991; Wiggins, 1989; Wolf, Bixby, Glenn, & Gardner, 1991). Students are asked to write essays, solve open-ended mathematical problems, communicate the reasons for their answers, engage in scientific experiments, and report on their findings. These kinds of assessments address higher-level thinking skills as well as more basic skills and provide information about student learning that supports instruction.

Moreover, these assessments occur in the context of actual classroom experience. Assessment is not thought of as a snapshot taken out of context, but as a collection of patterns of behavior and thinking over time (Wiggins, 1989). Such an approach to assessment takes into account the curriculum and instructional activities that provide students with the opportunities to develop their understanding, knowledge, and skills. These assessments also draw attention to individual students' strengths, weaknesses, preferences, interests, styles, and previous knowledge. When performance-based assessments are continuous and are used to monitor student learning longitudinally, they have the potential to improve instruction by closely linking instruction and assessment (Meisels, 1997; Meisels, Dorfman, & Steele, 1995). The Work Sampling System (Meisels, Jablon, Marsden, Dichtelmiller, & Dorfman, 2001) is an exemplar of this type of performance assessment. In fact, it is best described as an *instructional assessment.*

D.   The Work Sampling System

The Work Sampling System, an authentic performance assessment for preschool (3-year-olds)–grade 5, replaces the potentially misleading, out-of-context information obtained from conventional readiness and achievement tests with rich, dynamic data about how children respond to real classroom tasks and actual life situations. Work Sampling offers a comprehensive means of monitoring children's social, emotional, physical, and academic progress. It is an instructional assessment that is based on teachers' observations of children who are actively working and creating products day to day within the context of their daily classroom experience.

The purpose of the Work Sampling System is to document and assess children's skills, knowledge, behavior, and accomplishments across a wide variety of classroom activities and areas of learning on multiple occasions. It consists of three complementary elements: (1) teacher's observations informed by *Developmental Guidelines* and recorded on *Developmental Checklists;* (2) regular collection of children's work in *Portfolios;* and (3) teacher summaries of this information on *Summary Reports* each fall, winter, and spring. (See Appendix A for definitions of new terms.)

These elements are all classroom focused and instructionally relevant, reflecting the objectives of the classroom teacher. Instead of providing a mere snapshot of narrow academic skills at a single point in time, the elements of the System work together to create an ongoing evaluation process designed to improve both the student's learning and the teacher's instructional practices.

One of Work Sampling's strengths is its systematic structure. This structure allows teachers to collect extensive information from multiple sources and to use this information to evaluate what children know and can do. In its reliance on observing, collecting, and summarizing, Work Sampling organizes the assessment process so that it is both comprehensive in scope and manageable for teachers and students. We describe the mechanisms for observing, collecting, and summarizing below. (Appendix B contains a brief overview of Work Sampling.)

The *Developmental Guidelines* provide a framework for observation. They give teachers a set of observational criteria that are based on national standards and current knowledge of child development, such as those produced by the National Council of Teachers of Mathematics and the American Association for the Advancement of Science. In addition, they are consistent with proposals published by the National Education Goals Panel and others, and with the provisions for developmentally appropriate practices put forth by the National Association for the Education of Young Children. The Guidelines set forth developmentally appropriate expectations for children at each age or grade level. In using the Guidelines as the basis for their professional judgments, teachers in different settings can make decisions about children's behavior, knowledge, and accomplishments using identical criteria. Teachers record their observations on the *Developmental Checklists*.

Portfolios are purposeful collections of children's work that illustrate children's efforts, progress, and achievements. These collections are intended to display the individual nature and quality of children's work and their progress over time. Work Sampling advocates a structured approach to portfolio collection through the collection of two types of work samples: Core Items and Individualized Items. Core Items are designed to show growth over time by representing the same area of learning on three separate occasions during the school year. Individualized Items are designed to portray the unique characteristics of the child and to reflect work that integrates many domains of the curriculum. Child and teacher are both involved in the design, selection, and evaluation of Portfolios.

Summary Reports are completed three times a year. Teachers combine information from the Developmental Checklists and Portfolios with their own knowledge of child development to make evaluative decisions about student performance and progress. They summarize their knowledge of the child as they make ratings and write brief comments describing the student's strengths and their own areas of concern. Summary Reports take the place of conventional report cards.

The Work Sampling System addresses seven categories, or *domains*, of classroom learning and experience. These seven domains are as follows:

> **I. Personal and Social Development.** This domain emphasizes emotional and social competence. A teacher learns about children's emotional development—their sense of responsibility to

themselves and others, how they feel about themselves and view themselves as learners—through ongoing observation, conversations with children, and information from family members. Teachers learn about children's social competence by interacting with them, by observing their interactions with other adults and peers, and by watching how they make decisions and solve social problems.

II. Language and Literacy. This domain organizes the language and literacy skills needed to understand and convey meaning into four components: Listening, Speaking, Reading, and Writing. Students acquire proficiency in this domain through extensive experience with language, print, and literature in a variety of contexts. Over time students learn to construct meaning, make connections to their own lives, and gradually begin to critically analyze and interpret what they hear, observe, and read. They begin to communicate effectively both orally and in writing for different audiences and purposes.

III. Mathematical Thinking. The focus in this domain is on children's approaches to mathematical thinking and problem-solving. Emphasis is placed on how students acquire and use strategies to perceive, understand, and solve mathematical problems. Mathematics is about patterns and relationships, and about seeking multiple solutions to problems. In this domain, the content of mathematics (concepts and procedures) is stressed, but the larger context of understanding and application (knowing and doing) is also of great importance.

IV. Scientific Thinking. This domain addresses central areas of scientific investigation: inquiry skills and the physical, life, and earth sciences. The processes of scientific investigation are emphasized throughout because process skills are embedded in—and fundamental to—all science instruction and content. The domain's focus is on how children actively investigate through observing, recording, describing, questioning, forming explanations, and drawing conclusions.

V. Social Studies. Encompassing history, economics, citizenship, and geography, the domain of social studies emphasizes social and cultural understanding. Children acquire this understanding through personal experiences and from the experiences of others. As children study present day and historical topics, they learn about human interdependence and the relationships between people and their environment. Throughout social studies, children use a variety of skills, including conducting research, using oral and visual sources, solving problems systematically, and making informed decisions using the democratic process.

VI. The Arts. The emphasis in this domain is on children's engagement with the arts (dance, dramatics, music, and fine arts), both actively and receptively, rather than mastery of skills and techniques related to particular artistic media. The components address two ideas: how children use the arts to express, represent, and integrate their experiences, and how children develop an understanding and appreciation for the arts. It focuses on how opportunities to use and appreciate the arts enable children to demonstrate what they know, expand their thinking, and make connections among the arts, culture, history, and other domains.

VII. Physical Development and Health. The emphasis in this domain is on physical development as an integral part of children's well-being and educational growth. The components address gross motor skills, fine motor skills, and personal health and safety. A principal focus in gross motor is on children's ability to move in ways that demonstrate control, balance, and coordination. Fine motor skills are equally important in laying the groundwork for artistic expression, handwriting, and self-care skills. The third component addresses children's growing ability to understand and manage their personal health and safety.

Work Sampling not only provides the teacher with clear criteria for evaluation but also incorporates the teacher's own expertise and judgment. It is an evaluation system that does not dictate curriculum or instructional methods and that is designed for use with diverse groups of children in a variety of settings. The Work Sampling System is a flexible framework for assessment that helps teachers structure their assessments systematically and that encourages teachers to devise techniques best suited to their styles, their students, and their contexts.

Although the three elements of the Work Sampling System (Guidelines, Portfolios, and Summary Reports) can be used separately, they do form an integrated whole that draws upon teachers' perceptions of students while informing, expanding, and structuring those perceptions. The System allows teachers to assess children's development and accomplishments—rather than their test-taking skills—in meaningful, curriculum-based activities. It enables them to recognize and nurture children's unique learning styles, instead of rigidly classifying children as high- or low-achievers based on simplistic assessments. It also enables families to become actively involved in the assessment process. By objectively documenting what children learn and how teachers teach, Work Sampling provides for meaningful evaluation and genuine accountability. In addition, the Work Sampling System's comprehensive design provides a structure to foster the professional development of prospective teachers.

E. The Work Sampling System and Teacher Preparation

Using the Work Sampling System in your preservice program will foster your development in several ways. The *Developmental Guidelines* can be used to help you learn to make reasoned decisions—decisions that are based on evidence drawn from both theory and practice. As you learn to conduct focused, systematic, and unbiased observations, you will begin to appreciate the importance of collecting quality evidence and how essential this evidence is for making informed, reasoned instructional and assessment decisions (see Chapter 2). The Work Sampling System Portfolio can help you refine your ideas about what you want children to learn and how you will concretely document that learning. As you refine these ideas, you will see more clearly the connections among teaching, learning, and curriculum (see Chapter 3). Learning to write Summary Reports can help you gain a deeper understanding of assessment and evaluation as you practice writing narratives that portray children's learning. This will help you refine your ability to reflect on practice; you will be faced with the need to consider the purposes of assessment, how to evaluate performance, and how to communicate with families (see Chapter 4). You will begin to understand how instructional assessment is an essential aspect of responsible teaching, you will consider the broader goals and purposes of schools and schooling, and you will develop an awareness of an educator's responsibility to meet the multiple needs of each child.

Using the Work Sampling System can also help you track your own development as professionals. The assignments in this book provide a window into your thinking, illuminating how you are beginning to think like teachers. These assignments can serve as a method of self-assessment embedded in activities that help you understand how you will be expected to behave as professionals. If we accept that teaching is complex and ambiguous, we accept the necessity of this form of assessment, one that focuses on thought processes as much as it does on what you know and know how to do. Because development, whether professional or personal, is a process and not an end point, longitudinal and continuous forms of assessment are necessary. We also need to go beyond assessing behaviors, knowledge, and skills to assessing thinking—how we frame problems, generate solutions to those problems, and use those choices to inform future thinking and action. The use of the Work Sampling System materials in teacher education programs provides this information in a variety of ways.

F.   *How This Book Is Organized*

This book has three organizing chapters, each of which focuses on a specific aspect of teaching, and each of which tells how a particular element of the Work Sampling System can be used to help you learn that aspect of teaching. In Chapter 2 we show how the *Developmental Guidelines* can help you develop observational skills and an understanding of the role that evidence plays in reasoned decisions. Chapter 3 uses the Work Sampling System Portfolio to help you learn how to document meaningful learning through the careful collection and examination of children's work. In Chapter 4 Summary Reports are used to help you develop an understanding of the distinctions between performance and progress, how teachers can draw together multiple sources of information to make instructional and assessment decisions, and how to write meaningful narratives that present assessment information to families.

Chapters 2, 3, and 4 have parallel organizational frameworks. We begin by providing an overview of the main topics and questions addressed in the chapter and follow that with an introductory section addressing the rationale for the chapter's focus and the relevance of Work Sampling. Next we discuss the chapter's key topics, with specific, annotated assignments for each topic. We have developed three types of assignments: in-class, out-of-class, and field assignments. Although these assignments often build on one another, they may be used individually as well. In general, the in-class assignment introduces the topic, the out-of-class assignment provides you with opportunities to reflect, and the field assignment helps you connect theory to practice. Many of the exercises in this book will be most effective if you work with a small group of your peers to share your ideas and thinking. The instructor will provide any specific material that is needed. Finally, we end each chapter with a summary.

G.   Getting the Most out of This Book

Although this book draws heavily from the Work Sampling System, it is not intended to prepare you to use Work Sampling as a form of performance assessment. Rather, it is intended to use Work Sampling as a means of helping you learn to observe in order to make reasoned decisions, document higher-level learning, assess learning in complex and meaningful ways, and understand the interactive nature of teaching and learning. Work Sampling provides a structure to foster this learning in a systematic and meaningful way.

All of the quotes used throughout the book are from preservice students in the first semester of a two-year teacher education program. The majority are college juniors, 19–20 years old. The quotes were taken from assignments they completed using Work Sampling materials and were extracted with their permission either from their observations of a child or classroom, from narrative reports they completed on a child they observed throughout the semester, or from their reflections on these observations and narrative reports. We believe students' words communicate how powerfully Work Sampling supports the development of professionalism. We hope you find them equally helpful as well.

References

Bransford, J. D., Brown, A. L., & Cocking, R. R. (Eds.) (1999). *How people learn: Brain, mind, experience, and school.* Washington, DC: National Academy Press.

Calfee, R. (1987). The school as a context for assessment of literacy. *The Reading Teacher* (40), 738–743.

Calfee, R. (1992). Authentic assessment of reading and writing in the elementary classroom. In M. J. Dreher & W. H. Slater (Eds.), *Elementary school literacy: Critical issues* (pp. 221–226). Norwood, MA: Christopher Gordon.

Darling-Hammond, L., & Wise, A. (1985). Beyond standardization: State standards and school improvement. *The Elementary School Journal, 85*, 315–336.

Fredriksen, N. (1984). The real test bias: Influences of testing on teaching and learning. *American Psychologist, 39*, 193–202.

Frederiksen, J. R., & Collins, A. (1989). A systems approach to educational testing. *Educational Researcher, 18*, 27–32.

Haladyna, T. M., Nolen, S. B., & Haas, N. S. (1991). Raising standardized achievement test scores and the origins of test score pollution. *Educational Researcher, 20* (5), 2–7.

Haney, W. (1991). We must take care: Fitting assessment to functions. In V. Perrone (Ed.), *Expanding student assessment* (pp. 142–163). Alexandria, VA: Association for Supervision and Curriculum Development.

Koretz, D. (1988). Arriving in Lake Wobegone: Are standardized tests exaggerating achievement and distorting instruction? *American Educator, 12* (8–15), 46–52.

Lieberman, A. (1996). Networks and Reform in American Education. *Teachers College Record, 1*, 7–45.

Linn, R. L. (1987). Accountability: The comparison of educational systems and the quality of test results. *Educational Policy, 1*, 181–198.

Linn, R. L. (2000). Assessments and accountability. *Educational Researcher, 29*, 4–15.

Mehrens, W. A. (1992). Using performance assessment for accountability purposes. *Educational Measurement: Issues and Practice, 11* (3–9), 20.

Mehrens, W. A., & Kaminski, J. (1989). Methods for improving standardized test scores: Fruitful, fruitless, or fraudulent? *Educational Measurement: Issues and Practice, 8*, 14–22.

Meisels, S. J. (1989). High stakes testing in kindergarten. *Educational Leadership, 46*, 16–22.

Meisels, S. J. (1994). Designing meaningful measurements for early childhood. In B. L. Mallory & R. S. New (Eds.), *Diversity in early childhood education: A call for more inclusive theory, practice, and policy* (pp. 205–225). New York: Teachers College Press.

Meisels, S. J. (1997). Using Work Sampling in authentic assessments. *Educational Leadership, 54* (4), 60–65.

Meisels, S. J. (2000). On the side of the child: Personal reflections on testing, teaching, and early childhood education. *Young Children, 55* (6), 16–19.

Meisels, S. J., Dorfman, A., & Steele, D. (1995). Equity and excellence in group administered and performance-based assessments. In M. T. & A. L. Nettles (Eds.), *Equity and excellence in educational testing and assessment* (pp. 243–261). Boston, MA: Kluwer Academic Publishers.

Meisels, S. J., Jablon, J. R., Marsden, D. B., Dichtelmiller, M. L., & Dorfman, A. (2001). *The Work Sampling System* (4th ed.). Ann Arbor, MI: Rebus Inc.

Neill, D. M., & Medina, N. J. (1991). Standardized testing: Harmful to educational health. *Phi Delta Kappan, 73*, 688–697.

Paris, S. G., Lawton, T. A., Turner, J. C., & Roth, J. L. (1991). A developmental perspective on standardized achievement testing. *Educational Researcher, 20*(5), 12–20.

Shavelson, R. J., Baxter, G. P., & Pine, J. (1992). Performance assessments: Political rhetoric and measurement reality. *Educational Researcher, 21*, 22–27.

Shepard, L. A. (1989). Why we need better assessments. *Educational Leadership, 21*, 22–27.

Shepard, L. A. (1991). Interview on assessment issues. *Educational Researcher, 20*, 21–23; 27.

Shepard, L. A. (2000). The role of assessment in a learning culture. *Educational Researcher, 29* (7), 4–14.

Stiggins, R. J. (1991). Assessment literacy. *Phi Delta Kappan, 72* (7), 534–539.

Stiggins, R. J., Conklin, N. F., & Bridgeford, N. J. (1986). Classroom assessment: A key to effective education. *Educational Measurement: Issues and Practice, 5*, 5–17.

Urdan, T. C., & Paris, S. G. (1994). Teachers' perceptions of standardized achievement tests. *Educational Policy, 8* (2), 137–156.

Wiggins, G. (1989). A true test: Toward more authentic and equitable assessment. *Phi Delta Kappan, 70* (9), 703–713.

Wolf, D. P., & Reardon, S. (1996). Access to excellence through new forms of student assessment. In J. B. Baron & D. P. Wolf (Eds.), *Performance-based student assessment: Challenges and possibilities* (95th Yearbook of the Society for the Study of Education, pp. 1–31). Chicago, IL: Society for the Study of Education.

Wolf, D. P., Bixby, J., Glenn, J., & Gardner, H. (1991). *To use their minds well: Investigating new forms of student assessment.* Washington, DC: American Educational Research Association.

CHAPTER 2

Observing Learners and Learning

Focused and systematic observation plays a major role in teachers' work. In this chapter we discuss how you can come to understand that role. Specifically, we use the Work Sampling System *Developmental Guidelines* to help you learn to observe children's learning effectively. The *Guidelines* provide a structure that will help you develop a professional understanding of learners and learning. They illustrate what and how educators want children to learn and illuminate factors that may influence your understanding of children's behaviors. The assignments in this chapter take advantage of these characteristics of the *Guidelines* and apply them to the development of your observation skills.

A. *Introduction to Observation and the* Guidelines

Observing children's learning is one of the most important aspects of teaching. Through observation educators come to understand what children know, how they learn, and how to design instruction to foster further learning. The ways children approach tasks, ask questions, use materials, and interact with others provide evidence that educators can use to document learning and inform instruction (Drummond, 1994). Real insight into students' learning grows from repeated, ongoing, documented observation, rather than from the quick perusal of answers on worksheets or multiple-choice tests. However, effective observation and the ability to document learning do not develop on their own. In fact some educators never master these skills: their observations remain biased and unfocused, their documentation of learning limited and unduly subjective. For most educators the ability to observe and document learning effectively develops only through focused, thoughtful effort and ongoing experience.

Developing the skill of accurate and effective observation is not something to be left to chance—it should be a goal of all educators. Your observations as you enter your teacher preparation program, however, will often be influenced by beliefs, interpretations, and value judgments that you have not examined (Richardson, 1996). Your limited teaching experience and understanding of learners and learning may lead you to overgeneralize and to draw unsupported conclusions about what you are seeing when observing learners and learning in classrooms. Understanding the importance of focused, systematic, and unbiased observation is essential to your development as an effective and responsible educator. The Work Sampling System *Guidelines* provide a structure to help you learn how to observe effectively.

Five characteristics of the *Guidelines* contribute to the process of learning to observe. First, the *Guidelines* provide a structure for the observation of student learning. Seven broad curricular areas, or *domains*, at each age or grade level provide a focus for observations. These domains are Personal and Social Development, Language and Literacy, Mathematical Thinking, Scientific Thinking, Social Studies, the Arts, and Physical Development. These are the domains that most early childhood and elementary teachers are responsible for teaching.

Second, the *Guidelines* provide a portrait of classroom curricular activities. They illuminate what learning in different domains looks like, and they offer explicit guidance regarding what can be expected of learners at different age or grade levels in relation to the subject matter being taught. Each of the seven domains is divided into several subsets, or *functional components*. These will provide you with a deeper understanding of what learners are expected to master in different subject areas at different grade levels. They also provide insight into the substantive and syntactic (Schwab, 1978) nature of each learning domain. That is, each domain reflects the "big ideas" in what students are learning and how those ideas are related to and support other ideas in the domain. For example, Mathematical Thinking comprises the following functional components: approach to mathematical thinking, patterns and relationships, number concepts and operations, geometry and spatial relationships, measurement, and probability and statistics. Thinking mathematically means being able to think about patterns and relationships. Thinking mathematically about patterns and relationships means being able to see the patterns and relationships in numbers or measurement or geometry and how each is related to the other.

Third, through a given set of examples, the *Guidelines* provide insight into the multiple ways students approach and represent learning in each domain. Each functional component comprises a set of *performance indicators*. Performance indicators are skills, behaviors, attitudes, or accomplishments that can be observed and evaluated within the classroom. In the domain of Personal and Social Development at the third grade, for example, the functional components are self-concept, self-control, approaches to learning, interaction with others, and conflict resolution. Under the functional component of self-control, the performance indicators are follows classroom rules and routines, uses materials purposefully and respectfully, and manages transitions and adjusts behavior to new places and unexpected events. If, as a teacher, you are trying to determine if a particular student is developing self-control you could look for changes in how the student follows classroom rules and routines, uses materials, and manages transitions. Performance indicators help to focus observations—they tell a teacher what to look at to gain a full understanding of children's learning. They are used to provide multiple foci for a teacher's observations over time and across activities. The functional components and performance indicators for the Language and Literacy domain (first grade) are shown in Figure 2.1.

Fourth, the *Guidelines* provide an understanding of the continuous nature of children's thinking and development across grade levels. Although performance indicators are specific to each grade level, when looked at across grade levels they can help you better understand how learners acquire, develop, and demonstrate what they are learning year by year as they move through school. The *Guidelines* present six years of growth and development for each indicator, a progression that enables educators to place children's behavior and work into a longitudinal perspective. Here are one preservice teacher's reflections on her observations of a third-grade child:

> I think that, in terms of his self-concept, Joe seems to be closer to the first-grade level. For example, after writing a poem, he refused to read it in class or let the teacher read it because he did not think it was good

FIGURE 2.1   First-Grade Checklist Structure

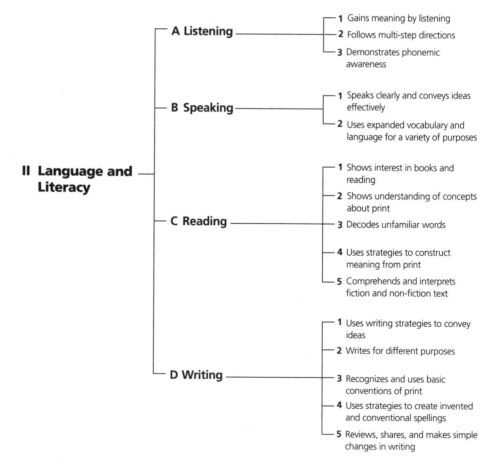

enough. He also avoids some of the children and sticks with his two friends because this is comfortable. Also, Joe has trouble locating specific materials for the appropriate activity.

This comment gives you a sense of the importance of a developmental perspective. The *Guidelines* provide one developmental framework for understanding learners and learning. As teachers, you will be presented with multiple guidelines including curriculum guidelines adopted by the systems for which you work, guidelines developed for use with the instructional materials you select, and guidelines generated in your mind from what you learn in your teacher preparation program and from experiences you have with children. The Work Sampling System *Guidelines* provide a comprehensive, detailed way to look at and understand children's learning in the range of subjects taught in elementary classrooms.

Finally, the *Guidelines'* performance indicators serve as measures of what children should be learning. The *Guidelines* incorporate national standards of curriculum development and teaching practice from such groups as the National Council of Teachers of Mathematics and the American Association for the Advancement of Science. In addition, they are consistent with proposals published by the National Education Goals Panel and others and with the provisions for developmentally appropriate practices put forth by the National Association for the Education of Young Children.

B.   *Learning How to Observe Learners and Learning*

Unless you become aware of the importance of learning how to observe, it is unlikely that focused, systematic, and unbiased observation will become an ongoing part of your practice. Without developing this skill it is also highly unlikely that you will be able to determine what qualifies as satisfactory evidence in reasoned, professional decision making. Understanding the importance of observation and evidence may be as critical as anything else you will learn in your teacher preparation program, and it may be as difficult as well. A lifetime of informal observation influences how you think about observation and how you approach the observation of children in classrooms (Lortie, 1975). As one preservice teacher noted, she still had "the tendency to observe things from the perspective of a camp counselor, checking to see if the students are involved in the activity and having fun." Time spent considering the role that observation plays in teaching can provide you with insight into what you know and believe about observation and can, in turn, sensitize you to factors that influence the process of observation.

Because many of you come to your teacher preparation program without a thorough understanding of the role that ongoing observation plays in a teacher's work, or of what can be learned from observing children in schools, becoming aware of the importance of observation is a necessary first step. Even when your preservice programs include directed observations, you may find yourself observing teachers or the context for teaching rather than learners and learning. You may also find yourself observing classroom management, classroom organization, curriculum implementation, or approaches to discipline. Although all of these foci are instructive, it is the observation of learners and learning that is central to teaching and one of the most difficult things to learn to do well. In our work we have found that even when preservice teachers begin by observing children, they often redirect those observations towards teachers. Although you may be more comfortable observing what is familiar to you—after all you have spent at least twelve years observing teachers in classrooms—it is essential to your future teaching to find effective ways to become comfortable with and effective at observing learners and learning. Preparation for observation also includes consideration of factors that contribute to accurate and reliable observations. Beginning to think about the issues of what to observe, how to observe, how to document your observations, and how to determine what they mean encourages you to begin to think like a teacher.

The following assignments are designed to help you become a teacher who observes children systematically and to address observation in general. The assignments ask you to: (1) consider the importance of observational techniques; (2) practice effective observation; and (3) identify barriers to effective observation. Your instructor may ask you to complete these assignments in sequence during consecutive class sessions, or they may be assigned as out-of-class reflective papers. Many of the assignments will be most effective if you work with a small group of your peers to share your ideas and thinking. Your instructor will provide any specific material that is needed. You may also be asked to return to these initial assignments as you refine your skills in observing learners in classrooms. In doing so you will be able to assess your developing skills in observation.

Exercise 2.1   What Does It Mean to Observe? (In-Class Assignment)

Background

Observation of children's actions, language, and the work they create in the context of classroom activities provides information about many aspects of their learning. Teachers who observe their students repeatedly, over time, and in a variety of classroom situations acquire a great deal of valid information that can guide their classroom decision making. Although becoming an effective, efficient, and accurate observer takes time, the first step is to understand the meaning and purposes of classroom observation.

Purposes

- To foster understanding of the importance of observation

- To heighten awareness of factors that contribute to accurate, reliable observations

Steps

1. As a large group, discuss the following:

   - What does it mean to observe?

   - What is its purpose?

   - How is it done?

   - When have you observed?

- What purpose does it serve in teaching?

2. In a small group, choose a facilitator who will keep the group on task and act as a time keeper, and a recorder who will keep track of your group's ideas.

3. Discuss each of the following questions, taking notes on your discussion:

- What can be learned from observing learners?

- Why is it important to observe students in context (in their natural environment)?

- Why is it important to do repeated observations?

- Why should observations be documented?

4. Be prepared to share your ideas with the large group.

Exercise 2.2   Learning Goals, Children's Activities, and Teaching Philosophy: Guides to Classroom Observation (In-Class Assignment)

Background

Effective observers understand the teacher's goals for children's learning and the relationship between those goals and classroom activities. Children learn most successfully when teachers provide activities that support the goals they have for children's learning. Some activities promote the development of specific skills, others support higher-order thinking and problem solving.

Purposes

- To encourage you to reflect upon the goals of teaching

- To help you consider the ways teaching goals are reflected in children's activities

- To increase awareness of the differences between skills-oriented teaching and teaching designed to develop higher-order thinking

Steps

1. In your small group, choose a facilitator who will keep the group on task and act as a time keeper, and a recorder who will keep track of the group's ideas.

2. Individually, think about learning goals for two or three specific children. List three to five goals that are most important for these children.

3. As a group, discuss the goals each person has listed. Identify the goals you share. Choose three to five goals that the group agrees are important for all children, and list them in order of priority.

4. Prepare to discuss one goal with the entire class. Consider the kind of learning that is reflected in the goal and how the goal can be measured. List some of the activities children might engage in as they pursue the goal.

5. Review your list of goals. Do different goals reflect different approaches to teaching? How?

6. Be prepared to share your ideas about one goal with the large group and to discuss the different approaches to teaching represented by various goals.

Exercise 2.3   How Do Children Show What They Know? (In-Class Assignment)

Background

Children demonstrate what they can do in many ways. Teachers continually reflect on children's actions, language, and work to better understand their learning.

Purposes

- To help you identify the varied ways in which children demonstrate what they know

- To heighten your awareness of the need to continue to identify examples or illustrations of learning

Steps

1. Select one goal for group discussion from the list that your class has developed. Have one member of your group initial your choice on that list. This will ensure that each small group selects a different goal.

2. In your small group choose a facilitator who will keep the group on task and act as a time keeper, a recorder who will record the group's ideas, and a presenter to lead a discussion with the large group.

3. Select an age or grade level.

4. Discuss the following questions, writing your comments on the transparency.

   - What are the learning goal and grade level that you have identified?

- ■ What are some ways in which children of this age can demonstrate what they know and what they can do in relation to this specific learning goal? Give several examples or illustrations of children's learning in this area.

5. Be prepared to lead a discussion about the two questions. Also be prepared to get additional input from other members of your class and add this to your transparency.

Exercise 2.4   Descriptions, Interpretations, and Values (Out-of-Class and Field Assignment)

Background

An important aspect of learning to observe is distinguishing among descriptions, interpretations, and values. Descriptions are limited to what the observer actually sees—what is observed. Interpretations include the observer's views on what the observation means. Values add a dimension to the interpretation that entails a judgment of worth.

Purposes

■ To help you begin to distinguish among descriptions, interpretations, and value judgments

■ To apply these distinctions to classroom observations

Steps

1. Complete a twenty-minute classroom observation before the next class period. Bring two copies of your observational notes to that class.

2. Select a partner. Exchange observational notes and take a few minutes to read your partner's notes. As you read, record the following:

   ■ Specific examples of descriptions, interpretations, and values

   ■ Your reasons for classifying the examples as you did

3. Discuss your comments with your partner.

4. From your observations, select examples of each type of statement to share with the class.

Exercise 2.5 Observing and Interacting (Field Assignment)

Background

Observation does not have to be a passive activity. Most frequently teachers are interacting with students at the same time that they are observing their students' learning. Expressing interest in children's activities and inquiring about their actions are two ways to gain additional information about their thinking.

Purposes

- To help you experience the complexity of observation when it occurs while interacting with children

- To help you develop techniques for eliciting information from children

Steps

1. Turn to someone sitting next to you and take a few minutes to talk about your experiences observing children. What challenges did you face? What questions remain about how to observe effectively?

2. Share your conversation with the class.

3. Discuss the following questions about observing and interacting with students simultaneously.

   - How can you elicit information from children?

   - What types of questions do children answer most readily?

- How can you show children that you are truly interested in their ideas?

4. Set up a classroom visit to observe one or two children in order to understand a child's perception of her own activities by interacting with the child. For example, if two children are building with blocks, what are they making and why? If a child is completing a math assignment, how is she making decisions about what to do?

5. Turn in your raw observational notes as well as a brief paper. The focus of the paper is to be on the observational process itself. Include responses to the following questions.

- What did you learn about participant observation?

- Did you change your techniques for documenting what you saw?

- What worked and what did not work?

- Did you think it was helpful to interact with the child, rather than just watching the child? Why?

- What kind of adjustments would you make the next time?

- What barriers did you encounter?

C. *Learning How to Conduct Focused Observations*

Although understanding the important role that observation plays in a teacher's work may foster your commitment to ongoing, focused observations in your own teaching, if you are to act on that commitment you must develop the necessary skills. A multitude of factors influence a teacher's ability to conduct focused observations. Classrooms are complex environments with multiple events occurring simultaneously. As a preservice student put it:

> Throughout this term, I have realized how difficult it is for teachers to observe all of their students and determine how they are developing on an individual level. It was extremely difficult for me to observe Joe because all of the other children were constantly coming up to me with questions and problems that needed to be addressed. I can only imagine how difficult it is for classroom teachers to find time to observe each child individually and assess their progress.

Events in classrooms are overlapping, multidimensional, and simultaneous (Doyle, 1983). For observation to be effective it must be focused. This means it must be conducted for a specific purpose, in a particular setting, and with particular learners in mind. At any moment in a classroom some children may be working independently on math while others are working in small reading groups, and still others are working individually with the teacher on a task they find difficult. Alternatively, although all children appear to be engaged in the same task, they may be engaged in the task in very different ways. Some children may be working on material that challenges them, others on material that is not interesting to them, and still others on material they find overwhelming. In addition, two children may be manifesting the same behavior but trying to express different meanings, whereas other children may be using different behaviors to communicate the same meaning (Drummond, 1994). Distinguishing among these different possibilities requires careful, thoughtful observation. The *Guidelines* can help you learn to do so.

By providing a specific focus and helping you know what to look for, the Work Sampling System *Guidelines* can help you learn how to observe more effectively. The *Guidelines* provide a focus for what to watch for when children complete assignments, use materials, solve problems, and interact with others. The *Guideline's* domains, components, and indicators can be used for other, related purposes as well: (1) to guide the questions you ask children about their work; (2) to help you learn how to listen as children talk with others informally and during group discussions; and (3) to provide a structure for reviewing children's work (e.g., projects, writings, drawings, reports, math problems, learning logs, and journals). Using the *Guidelines* to structure your interactions with children helps you learn how to recognize and generate the evidence needed to make reasoned decisions about children as learners.

In addressing multiple domains and a wide range of age and grade levels, the *Guidelines* provide a breadth of understanding about children as learners as well as an in-depth understanding of how children's understanding grows and develops within those multiple domains and age or grade levels. They serve as a reminder of how important it is to observe *all* children in *all* domains; they provide a method for interpreting collections of observations; they help you learn how to summarize what you have seen; and they foster an understanding of fair, unbiased assessment. Using the *Guidelines* as you begin to observe learning and learners can also provide you with an understanding of the "warrants" or evidence that forms the foundation for the instructional decisions teachers make. Using the *Guidelines* as a framework, you will learn how to observe and document learning systematically and become sensitive to the importance of observing children's acquisition of skills, knowledge, and understanding across all areas of the curriculum, across time. The following assignments are designed to help you become more familiar with the *Guidelines* and begin to use them to focus your observations.

Exercise 2.6   Becoming Familiar with the *Developmental Guidelines* (In-Class Assignment)

Background

The Work Sampling System *Guidelines* can help you observe children more effectively by providing you with specific areas on which to focus. They can help you know what to look for as you observe children learning. The *Guidelines* are organized into seven domains. Each domain is composed of several functional components. Each of these components is further divided into two to five performance indicators. There is a rationale for every performance indicator and several examples of the ways children demonstrate learning related to that performance indicator.

Purposes

- To give you an opportunity for hands-on exploration of the *Omnibus Guidelines*

- To let you become familiar with the vocabulary of the *Guidelines*

- To give you a chance to consider how the *Guidelines* can help you focus your observations of children's learning

Steps

1. In your small group, choose a facilitator who will keep the group on task and act as a time keeper, and a recorder who will keep track of the group's ideas.

2. Take a few minutes to review the organization of the *Guidelines*. Find the seven different domains. Look for the components, indicators, rationales, and examples for each of the domains.

3. In your small group, without using the *Guidelines*, generate a list of personal and social development goals for children. Base your list upon observations you have made in classrooms or of children you know.

4. Try to find these goals in the *Guidelines*.

5. Discuss the rationales and examples below the indicators that support these goals.

6. Generate a list of other examples of the indicators you are discussing.

7. Be prepared to join the rest of the class for a general discussion about the *Guidelines* focusing on the following questions:

   ■ Were you able to locate your personal and social goals in the *Guidelines*?

   ■ Give an example you developed to add to the *Guidelines*.

   ■ What were your overall reactions to the *Guidelines*?

   ■ Did issues come up in your discussions that have not been mentioned?

Exercise 2.7   Observing for Indicators of Learning (Out-of-Class and Field Assignment)

Background

The *Guidelines* contain indicators for every component of the domains. Indicators that seem fairly straightforward when discussed in class may become less clear when you attempt to match them up with what you are observing. In this assignment you will observe a child for a specific indicator. The indicator has been identified for you.

Purposes

- To help you better understand the *Guidelines*

- To help you become more familiar with the indicators in the *Guidelines*

- To help you learn how to observe for a specific indicator

Steps

Before the Out-of-Class Observation

1. Discuss the following questions in relation to the indicator that has been assigned to you.

   - What does the indicator mean to you?

   - When can it be observed?

   - How might it be observed?

2. In your small group, develop a plan for observing a child for this indicator. Be sure to answer these questions:

- Who will you observe?

- Where will you observe?

- When will you observe?

3. Conduct an observation sometime before the next class meeting and document that observation in writing.

4. Be ready to share your observations in class with a partner.

After the Out-of-Class Observation

1. Work with a partner to review and critique each other's work. During your critique consider the following:

- Does the documentation provide sufficient evidence of the indicator?

■ What are the possible biases that may have influenced the observation?

■ What are the possible limitations of such a "one-shot" observation?

2. Be prepared to share your discussion with the large group.

Exercise 2.8   Understanding the Multiple Ways Learning Is Represented (Field Assignment)

Background

Children demonstrate their learning in multiple ways. The *Guidelines* offer many examples of how children demonstrate the same aspect of learning within and across age and grade levels. Before our next class you will be expected to complete an observation of a child that concentrates on the domain and component of learning that we have identified in class.

Purposes

- To provide you with opportunities to observe and discuss the various ways the same aspect of learning may be demonstrated within and across age and grade levels in the *Guidelines*

- To give you a sense of the multiple ways children represent what they know

Steps

Before the Out-of-Class Observation

1. As a group, we will select a domain and a component of children's learning that all students will observe. Please consider the following as you plan for conducting your observation:

   - The rationale, indicators, and illustrations of the selected component

   - The similarities and differences in the indicators of that component of learning across age/grade levels

   - Examples other than those listed in the *Guidelines*

2. In your small group, plan your observation.

3. Record your small group discussions. These will be reviewed during the next class.

4. Conduct your observation before the next class meeting.

After the Out-of-Class Observation

1. Meet in small groups by age and grade levels. Share your observations in preparation for discussion with the full group. Discuss and reflect on the following:

   - Agreements or disagreements over whether the observations reflect the component

   - Similarities and differences in your observations

   - Difficulties encountered in observing the component

   - Whether the examples you observed would be appropriate examples at other grade levels and why or why not

   - The implications of your work for teaching and learning

D. *Becoming Systematic Observers*

Accurate and meaningful observations are systematic and comprehensive. In order to understand student learning in ways that inform instruction and assessment, teachers must observe learning over time and under a variety of conditions and must use a variety of techniques in systematic ways. In addition, they must have a clear understanding of what it is they are trying to observe. As prospective teachers this is a difficult challenge. You come to teacher education programs with a limited understanding of both the processes of learning and the subject matter children are learning. To gain insight into the variety of ways that children learn, you must first develop an understanding of how specific aspects of learning in particular domains can be conceptualized. For example, what do educators mean when they say a child is able to "read text fluently, independently, and for varied purposes"? What does "fluent" mean? What does it mean to "read independently"? How do teachers recognize fluent and independent reading? How do they document it? How do they use that information to plan instruction?

As prospective teachers you also must come to understand the comprehensive nature of the evidence that is needed to answer these kinds of questions and to make instructional decisions. Understanding the learning that is being observed is not sufficient. Thoughtful educators who make reasoned decisions are also able to present a substantive body of evidence regarding the decisions they make. The evidence that practicing teachers collect is diverse, ranging from practical experience to formal research (Fenstermacher, 1994). But no evidence is more important to practice than the evidence provided through the systematic observation of learners in the classroom. The Work Sampling *Guidelines* can help you gain a deeper understanding of learning and of the evidence for teachers' decision making by focusing on the systematic data required for this approach to understanding your students as learners. Moreover, the importance of repeated observations over time and of documenting the context of the observations (Cazden & Mehan, 1989) is highlighted by the *Guidelines*. Here is a preservice teacher's reflection on the importance of context when observing in classrooms:

> I feel I have accomplished a great deal in simply developing an acceptance and understanding of the classroom environment. This important step allowed me to see the child within the context of the school rather than within my own context of what education should look like, as in a more traditional classroom filled with desks, homework, and textbooks.

As prospective teachers you can use the *Guidelines* to come to understand how making judgments about a child's learning based on limited observations ignores the complexity in learning and obscures the multiple factors that may influence a learner's performance. In doing so, you will be better able to avoid making limited observations in your own practice and therefore meet the needs of all of your students more effectively and equitably.

Your engagement with and reflection on repeated, focused observations of specific aspects of learning will help you acquire critical insights into teaching. In particular, you will come to understand that before you can conduct observations that accurately and reliably document learning, you must first become aware of those factors that interfere with your ability to observe a learner fairly. For example, one student writes of reading her own situation into that of the child's:

> Before I "empathize" with the idea that Kayla is being rejected, I should reflect on the idea that Kayla's culture could play a great role in the way I perceive her social interaction. As an Asian, Kayla may be more reserved in conversation than are many other children. She may, in fact, be quite comfortable with the way things are. I could have been digging too deeply within my initial observation to find something wrong with the situation because of previous experiences that have affected me as a minority student.

As students of teaching, you must learn to reserve judgment, focus your observations, document in detail what each learner is doing, and collect sufficient evidence to develop a reasoned understanding of individual learners. The *Guidelines* can prompt you to begin thinking in these ways—to reason like professionals, to think like teachers. The assignments that follow use the *Guidelines* to help you learn how to plan for the *systematic* observation of learning. They are designed to help you better understand the nature of systematic observations by making you aware of the importance of clearly conceptualizing aspects of learning, by helping you determine when you have sufficient evidence to make decisions about student learning, and by showing you how to develop a formal plan for observation.

Exercise 2.9   Thinking about Aspects of Learning (In-Class Assignment)

Background

Focusing on limited aspects of student learning each time you observe will help you develop an in-depth understanding of the *Guidelines*. Moreover, limiting what you are looking for will heighten your awareness of how factors extraneous to the classroom may influence your observations. This in-class assignment is designed to help you explore your own assumptions and beliefs and how they may affect your interpretations of the *Guidelines*.

Purposes

- To help you appreciate the necessity for observing with a clear focus

- To help you understand how your own assumptions and beliefs influence your observations and interpretations of the *Guidelines*

Steps

1. In your small group, discuss the component of self-concept, taking notes on your discussion. Use the following questions to guide your discussion.

   - What is self-concept?

   - How do children of different ages demonstrate self-concept?

   - What does it mean to say a child has a good self-concept? a poor self-concept?

   - Why do teachers care about children's self-concept?

2. After you have discussed these questions, read the pages in the *Omnibus Guidelines* about self-concept.

3. Answer each question again. Note the similarities and differences between your prior knowledge and assumptions about self-concept and the information in the *Guidelines*.

4. Discuss what you can do to keep your own assumptions from biasing your observations. Think about how you will know when you have sufficient evidence about a child's self-concept to make a judgment about it.

5. Be prepared to share your discussions with the large group.

Exercise 2.10   When Is the Evidence Sufficient? (Out-of-Class and Field Assignment)

Background

Over the past several weeks, we have discussed classroom observation from a conceptual perspective. In order to be an effective observer, you must have a plan for observation and must observe repeatedly, interpret your observations, and determine when you have sufficient evidence to make an evaluative judgment. In this activity, you will work with a partner or in a small group focusing on one component from the *Guidelines*. You will develop, implement, and evaluate a plan for observation of one component and one child.

Purposes

- To give you a chance to develop and implement a focused plan for observation

- To help you learn to interpret observations

- To allow you to explore the question of how much evidence is sufficient

Steps

As a Group

1. In your pair or small group, identify the *Guidelines* domain and component of learning that you will observe. Note how you reach this decision.

2. Discuss and develop a clear conceptualization of the component you chose.

3. Identify possible biases in how you conceptualize the component.

4. Identify the specific child that you will observe, and share with other students your reasons for selecting that child.

5. Plan when you will observe and why you have selected that time during the day.

6. Identify what the evidence might look like and the best documentation methods and tools for capturing it. Are you likely to see the child working alone or interacting with others? Will you take anecdotal notes, collect some of the child's work, use a tally, or record a language sample? These are just some examples of the types of data you might collect.

7. Discuss how you will determine if and when you have sufficient evidence to draw conclusions about this component for this child.

8. Critique one another's plans and modify them accordingly.

Individually

9. Conduct repeated observations over time, observing for the component that you have identified. Write a summary of your observations. Describe enough of the context so that another person can make sense of your observational notes.

With a Partner

10. Exchange papers with someone in your small group to critique your experience by addressing each issue raised above.

Individually

11. Complete a short reflection paper addressing why evidence is important to teacher decision making and how a teacher knows when he has sufficient evidence to make a decision.

12. Turn in your observational notes and summaries with the reflection paper.

Exercise 2.11   Managing Systematic Observations (In-Class and Field Assignment)

Background

When people think of observing children in classrooms, they often envision a teacher who is physically separated from her students, writing lengthy anecdotal notes on a clipboard. That type of observation, however—when teachers step out of the action and record what they see—happens only infrequently in classrooms. More frequently teachers observe and record their observations while they are in the midst of the classroom action: when they are leading activities, giving directions, and interacting with children. It is important, then, that teachers have a variety of ways to record quickly and efficiently what they see and hear.

Purposes

- To help you gain awareness of observational methods

- To help you gain awareness of observational tools

- To give you experience using two to three different observational methods

Steps

1. Read the handouts on observational approaches, methods, and tools that are included in Appendix C.

2. Discuss how a teacher might decide whether to observe in the action, out of the action, or after the fact.

3. Review the examples of observations documented in different ways. Discuss why a teacher might decide to use a tally, time sampling, or an anecdotal record. Do different methods give different information about children? Do they demand different things from teachers?

4. After reading the handout on observational tools, brainstorm a list of observational tools that you might use.

5. Before the next class session, observe and document your observations for fifteen minutes when you are interacting with children. You might be leading an activity, interacting informally with children, or playing a game. This will give you a more accurate picture of classroom observation than will the observation you conducted previously by stepping out of the action.

6. Conduct the observation using two different observational methods. For example, you might use a tally to gather data about some behaviors and use a matrix to capture other information during the same classroom visit.

7. During the next class session, discuss your experiences observing while you were interacting with students. How did this type of observation differ from the observations you conducted previously? Were your perceptions changed in any way?

Exercise 2.12   A Teacher's Journal (Field Assignment)

Background

This is an ongoing assignment that is intended to help you integrate your knowledge about observation and to link this knowledge to practice. To complete it, you will need to observe one child or a group of children systematically over an extended period of time in an early childhood or elementary school classroom.

Purposes

- To give you practice observing systematically and with a focus

- To help you gain awareness of the relationship between the focus of observation and the methods and tools used to document observations

- To allow you to reflect critically on the process of observing and documenting learning and learners

Steps

1. Determine whether you will observe one student, one domain, or a classroom activity (e.g., math time or free choice time) as the focus of this activity.

2. Conduct these observations at least twice a week for several weeks.

3. Experiment with a variety of ways of observing (e.g., in the action or out of the action), documentation methods, and documentation tools.

4. Each time you leave the classroom, summarize your observations. Note questions about the child, domain, or activity. Describe your initial interpretations based on your observations.

5. Keep your original observational notes and your journal that summarizes your observations, questions, and interpretations.

6. Write reflection papers as assigned in class.

E. Conducting Unbiased Observations

Prior beliefs, expectations, and values that potentially bias what educators see and document, or even what they choose to observe and document can undermine observations that are focused and systematic. Teachers' expectations for learners may be based on factors that have little in common with the learners' actual performance. Factors related to individual children such as gender, race, culture, language, or family socioeconomic status may influence what a teacher sees or chooses to see. Prior experience with a student's siblings or families may direct observations in ways that lead to a biased understanding of the student as a learner. To attempt to counteract these influences, teachers can try consciously to view the child from other perspectives. They can try to understand how families might see and interpret the child's performance and how the performance might be viewed from the child's perspective.

Factors in teachers' lives may influence how they observe and document student learning. A teacher's expectations for students, when based on the teacher's own cultural background and experience, may have a limited appreciation for how students from other cultures demonstrate, for example, "eagerness and curiosity as a learner." The following is a reflection written by a preservice student beginning the process of identifying her own potential observational biases.

My brother was diagnosed with ADD [Attention Deficit Disorder] just a little over a year ago and was prescribed Ritalin. . . . Simply because of my prior knowledge of this problem there are certain traits that I tend to associate with a child with ADD . . . I tend to picture students with ADD as being very active all of the time. This assumption caused me many difficulties when observing John. Several times I found myself looking for traits in John which I assume to be typical of ADD students. For example, my mother told me that, at the clinic where my brother's diagnosis was done, the doctor told her that many children with ADD are extremely bright; however they score low on tests. When I learned John was placed last in the math group I assumed that he must be a "bright" kid who is a poor test taker.

A limited understanding of particular content areas may also bias a teacher's observation of a student in that area (McDiarmid, Ball, & Anderson, 1989). For example, if teachers do not have a strong background in mathematics, they will find it difficult to understand and appreciate the multiple ways learners may "communicate mathematical thinking through oral and written language." Effective and responsible teachers continually reflect on possible biases in their observations and interpretations and do what they can to overcome them.

Learning to conduct focused and systematic observations sensitizes you to the complexity of learning in multiple domains, discourages overgeneralization, and limits the possibility of bias. Using the *Guidelines* to focus your observations encourages you to attend to how children represent learning rather than to who the children are. The specificity provided by the domains, components, and indicators places the emphasis on what children can do, how they do it, and the conditions under which their accomplishments take place. The *Guidelines'* emphasis on the multiple ways learning is represented also encourages you, as prospective teachers, to see each child's individuality as a learner, and to be attentive to the individual ways that learners represent what they know and can do.

The *Guidelines* can help you become aware of factors that may bias your interpretations. They also facilitate your awareness of personal assumptions that may limit how you see different children, influence your interpretations of how children represent their learning, lead *you* to overgeneralize during your assessment of learning, and undermine your ability to educate effectively and responsibly. The structure, comprehensiveness, and standards on which the *Guidelines* are based provide a framework for understanding the evidence that justifies instructional practices and for developing the ability to observe, document, and assess learning in unbiased ways.

The assignments in this section are designed to encourage you to recognize and explore the sources of your own biases in order to control the influence of these sources on your interactions in classrooms and in instructional decisions. They also focus on helping you understand the complexity involved in observing and interpreting the behavior of diverse learners.

Exercise 2.13   How Clearly Do Teachers See Their Students? (In-Class Assignment)

Background

As a teacher, you will continually observe children's actions, language, and the work they produce in school. Your interpretations of these observations are an important source of information about their learning and will support your decision making. But sometimes teachers' perceptions of students are biased. Over time, teachers can learn to become less biased observers.

Purposes

- To help you identify possible biases that may influence observation

- To lead you to reflect on ways to move beyond possible biases

Steps

1. In your small group, choose a facilitator who will keep the group on task and act as a time keeper, and a recorder who will keep track of the group's ideas.

2. List the factors that you believe influence your perceptions in the classroom. In your discussion, consider factors about children, families, and teachers.

3. After you have listed factors in each category, discuss the following:

   - What is it about each factor that influences your perceptions?

   - How does it influence you?

- Which factors, listed by others, might affect you as well?

- How can you overcome some of these obstacles to unbiased observation?

4. Be prepared to share your ideas with the large group.

Exercise 2.14 Becoming More Aware of Biases (In-Class Assignment)

Background

A precondition for conducting unbiased observation is a recognition of one's own biases. Personal biases may limit your ability to see the richness and complexity of the children in your classroom as learners.

Purposes

- To help you begin to recognize your own personal biases

- To help you reflect on where your biases originate

- To help you see how biases may influence your teaching practice

Steps

1. In your small group, choose a recorder who will write down the group's ideas. The recorder will use the overhead projector marker to write on the blank transparency.

2. Brainstorm a list of factors (issues/concerns/perspectives) that can affect your perceptions of children.

3. Review the list and identify common categories or common themes for the words and phrases you have listed. Discuss how each category affects perceptions.

4. List the major points of your discussion on the transparency. Prepare to share your list with the class.

5. After all group presentations have been completed, you will be asked to reflect on:

- the most prevalent categories identified,

- factors you may not have considered and why,

- how you can control for biases, and

- how you can become sensitive to factors of which you are not yet aware.

Exercise 2.15   Learning to Recognize Our Own Biases by Writing an Educational Life History (Out-of-Class Assignment)

Background

For most of us, the task of exploring personal biases must take place privately. It is an exploration that requires memory, reflection, honesty, and thought. Honest reflection is not always best achieved or most easily accomplished in a group setting. This assignment is intended to help you explore the foundations for your personal biases.

Purposes

- To help you begin to explore the foundations of your personal biases

- To help you see how similar experiences can have different interpretations and outcomes

- To help you understand that similar experiences can influence future behavior in different ways

Steps

Write your educational life history. In this history address such issues and events as teachers and teaching, students and learning, subject matter, and context. During the next class we will discuss the beliefs and assumptions that each of us has and those which may limit our ability to meet the needs of all children effectively; we will ask you to share some of your own experiences. As you write your narrative you may find it helpful to think about such issues as these:

- What teaching approach worked most effectively with you?

- Do you think this approach would be equally effective for all learners?

- Why do you think some children seem to thrive under a particular teacher's instruction while others do not?

- What can teachers do to change their instruction?

- Was there a particular subject at which you were most successful? Least successful? Do you think those experiences may influence how you teach those subjects?

- Have your interpretations of your own educational experiences changed through your observations of children and discussions in the classroom? Explain how and in what ways.

Exercise 2.16   Controlling Biases (Field Assignment)

Background

Prospective teachers need practice in learning to distinguish between descriptions and interpretations and in how to control biases. Even when we are able to recognize and acknowledge some of our own biases, it is difficult to be aware of the variety of ways they may influence our thoughts and actions. One way of helping you accomplish this is by obtaining and using feedback from others.

Purposes

- To help you distinguish between observations and interpretations

- To help you learn to identify and control your own biases

- To help you become more sensitive to the power of your interpretations through obtaining and using feedback from others

Steps

1. Arrange another observation visit. During this visit you will record your observations in a manner that will give you practice in distinguishing between observations and interpretations.

2. Complete two sets of notes: descriptive notes, or what you observe, and interpretive notes, or what you think your observation means. The descriptive notes should be written while you are observing. The interpretive notes should be completed as soon as possible after the observation.

3. In the next class, share your descriptive notes only with another student. The other student will write an interpretation of the observation based on your description.

4. Discuss the differences in your interpretations, focusing on such factors as: (1) limitations in the observations; (2) limitations in the documentation provided; and (3) personal bias that may have influenced each of your interpretations.

5. Brainstorm ways to control for the limitations discussed by the two of you. Focus on how we can identify and control for our own biases.

F. *Summary*

Learning how to observe is one of the most important skills you can develop as a prospective teacher. Accurate and meaningful observations lay the foundation for understanding each of the learners in your classroom and for planning instruction that maximizes each child's potential. In this chapter we used the Work Sampling System *Guidelines* in a variety of ways to help you learn to observe in focused, systematic, and unbiased ways. As discussed, the first step in this process is becoming aware of the importance of observation. Addressing why observation is an important part of teaching, recognizing factors that are relevant to effective observation, and identifying barriers to effective observation sensitizes you, as a prospective teacher, to the importance of reasoned decision making and lays the foundation for your own observations.

To ensure that observations inform assessment and instructional decisions, your observations of children must be focused, systematic, and unbiased. The Work Sampling System *Guidelines* provide a structure for helping you learn how to do so. They help to make you more aware of the indicators of learning in multiple domains and to the multiple ways different students represent their learning. They encourage you, as well, to consider the importance of systematic observations. Systematic observations require a clear conceptualization of student learning, an awareness of the evidence necessary to make accurate and meaningful instructional and assessment decisions, and a well-designed plan of observation. Observations can be undermined, however, by bias. Experience conducting focused and systematic observations helps you become aware of and learn how to recognize and control your own biases.

The development of the ability to observe learning in focused, systematic, and unbiased ways is crucial to your development as an educator. This ability provides the foundation for your development as effective and responsible educators who make reasoned decisions on the basis of evidence. The assignments in this chapter were designed to help you understand how that evidence is grounded in observations and drawn from the work that children do. In the next chapter the Work Sampling System Portfolio is used to help you gain deeper insight into the various ways children represent their learning and how a teacher's goals are reflected in what children are asked to do. The assignments in that chapter draw from the Work Sampling System Portfolio and are designed to foster your understanding of the connections between teaching, learning, and assessment.

References

Ball, D., & Wilson, D. (1996). Integrity in teaching: Recognizing the fusion of the moral and the intellectual. *American Educational Research Journal, 33*(1), 155–192.

Cazden, C.B., & Mehan, H. (1989). Principles from sociology and anthropology: Context, code, classroom, and culture. In M. C. Reynolds (Ed.), *Knowledge base for the beginning teacher* (pp. 47–58). Washington, DC: Pergamon Press.

Doyle, W. (1983). Academic work. *Review of Educational Research 53*(2), 159–199.

Drummond, M. J. (1994). *Learning to see: Assessment through observation.* New York: Stenhouse.

Fenstermacher, G. (1994). The knower and the known: The nature of knowledge in research on teaching. In L. Darling-Hammond (Ed.), *Review of research in education, (vol. 20).* Washington, DC: American Educational Research Association.

Lortie, D. (1975). *Schoolteacher: A sociological study.* Chicago: University of Chicago Press.

McDiarmid, W. G., Ball, D. L., & Anderson, C. W. (1989). Why staying one chapter ahead doesn't really work: Subject-specific pedagogy. In M. C. Reynolds (Ed.), *Knowledge base for the beginning teacher* (pp. 193–206). Washington, DC: Pergamon Press.

Richardson, V. (1996). The role of attitudes and beliefs in learning to teach. In J. Sikula (Ed.), *Handbook of research on teacher education,* 2nd ed. (pp. 102–119). New York: MacMillan.

Schwab, J. (1978). Education and the structure of the disciplines. In I. Westbury & N. J. Wilkof (Eds.), *Science, curriculum, and liberal education* (pp. 229–272). Chicago: The University of Chicago Press.

CHAPTER 3

Documenting Meaningful Learning

In this chapter we discuss the importance of fostering meaningful learning in children and the ways in which, as teachers, you can document it. We use the Work Sampling System Portfolio to help you learn how to document meaningful learning as well as to develop an understanding of the connections between teaching, learning, and assessment. By focusing attention on the work in which children engage, portfolios expand and deepen our understanding of both teaching and learning.

A. *Introduction*

In order to understand what children know, understand, and think, teachers must study expressions of children's thoughts. These expressions are represented in multiple ways including their writing and language, how they think dramatically and artistically, and through their behavior. All of the work and activities in which children engage are means of expression that illustrate their thinking processes, as the following preservice teacher notes in her observation of a third grader:

> As I observed and listened in on the group, I noticed Kayla giving an answer for a problem to another student. I recalled the classroom teacher's rule of letting students assist one another as long as the student explained how to find the answer. Kayla's friend was having difficulty solving this story problem: *A man went to the store and purchased 29 apples, 121 pears, 5 oranges, and 36 bananas. How many pieces of fruit did the man buy?*
> I noticed the friend had written the problem in this way:
>
> 121
> 29
> 36
> 5
>
> I asked Kayla what was wrong with the problem. She explained to her friend the importance of numeric positioning according to the ones, tens, and hundreds in order to solve the problem.

This example illustrates how teachers must go beyond what children do and consider how they think and understand. As this preservice teacher learned, one child's representation of a story problem misled her but another child was able to comprehend and convey what needed to be changed in order for the problem to be solved successfully.

In order to understand children's thinking and its relationship to their learning, teachers must have a comprehensive understanding of the different ways children represent what they know in different subject area domains. Such understanding grows from teachers' involvement in teaching, learning, curriculum work, and assessment. Because you do not have that range of formal experience to draw from, helping you find ways to develop and refine your own understanding so that you can learn from children's work is the challenge of this chapter.

Portfolios, a relatively new approach to assessment in education, are purposeful collections of the learner's work. They can be used in a variety of ways, but generally are intended to create a portrait of a learner and to tell a story about the individual's learning and development over time. Portfolios used in schools document children's experience in school, illuminate how each child learns, and capture the quality of his or her work (Grace & Shores, 1991). Portfolios are also used in some teacher education programs. They may be used either as assessment tools or as professional portfolios, documenting prospective teachers' developing skills and understandings (Barton & Collins, 1993). Portfolios used with in-service teachers, such as those outlined in the National Board of Professional Teaching Standards (NBPTS) or the Interstate New Teacher Assessment and Support Consortium (INTASC), are used to assess and document a teacher's professional growth and development relative to established criteria and standards.

The Work Sampling System's definition of portfolios as "purposeful" most closely parallels the thinking reflected in the NBPTS and INTASC documents. Each is used for assessment and each reflects a high degree of purpose and structure. The guidelines provided with NBPTS, INTASC, and Work Sampling outline a focused strategy of collection and limit the number of items collected. The individuals being assessed are active participants in the process. The items selected for inclusion reflect the quality of the work and thought of the individual being assessed and are intended to document his or her thinking or comprehension in specific domains. One of the central tasks in all of these approaches is finding concrete ways to represent internal thought processes.

The Work Sampling System used during your teacher preparation program can help you to learn to meet the challenge of finding concrete ways to represent your students' internal thought processes when you become a practicing teacher. The Portfolio, in particular, offers a structure that provides a coherent and integrated understanding of the specific ways children's learning may be represented, how that learning can be assessed, and the implications for instruction and future learning. Whereas the *Guidelines* used in Chapter Two provided lenses to focus observations and insight into the evidence that supports assessment and instruction, the Portfolio prompts consideration of the various ways learning can be documented for different learners in different domains. Through the use of the Work Sampling System Portfolio you will be encouraged to develop the flexibility in thinking that is a hallmark of reflective practice and a necessary condition for fostering meaningful learning in all the children with whom you may work.

B.   Connecting Teaching, Learning, and Assessment

During the past decade the importance of fostering higher levels of understanding and thinking in all children has become increasingly apparent (Bransford, Brown, & Cocking, 1999; Cohen, McLaughlin, & Talbert, 1993). All children should be provided with opportunities to master all aspects of the curriculum. And all children must learn more than the basics if they are to succeed in a rapidly changing society. In order to accomplish these goals the learning opportunities that teachers provide for children must be grounded in comprehensive knowledge of subject matter and should be designed to facilitate children's conceptual understanding of the material. Teaching must go beyond the goal of getting children to memorize sets of facts to encouraging their understanding of the subjects being taught and their ability to draw from and build on what they have learned as they go through school. Although there will always be important educational goals and objectives that can be accomplished effectively in a procedural way, such as learning to spell or to multiply, higher levels of learning require that children's knowledge move beyond procedures to understanding the subjects, the basis of various procedures used in different subject areas, and the connections between both (Schwab, 1978; Tharp & Gallimore, 1988). For example, when teachers teach in this way, learners understand how regrouping is related to multiplication and what it means for this mathematical operation. They can tell the teacher and their classmates the rules they use to classify objects in the scientific domain, why they do so, and the implications for other learning. In short, their learning is meaningful. The following observation made by a preservice teacher suggests what and how children understand is as important as what they are able to do:

> Typically, the children are given two to three story problems to solve. Sometimes children will have difficulty answering the question. I assist them. My response usually is to point out the "given" statements. "Well, what do we already know?" They respond. "How do we know that?" They respond. "What then do you think we should do?" They respond. "Is that reasonable?" They respond. "How do we know it is/is not reasonable?" They respond. This series of questions and answers allows me to see what they already know, how they use this knowledge, and how they learn.

Teachers who are committed to fostering meaningful learning are aware that different subject areas—that is, different disciplinary domains—may require different pedagogies. The techniques and methods used to foster meaning in science are substantively different from the methods used in language and literacy. They also understand that different objectives within the same domain may require different pedagogical approaches. The approach used to foster children's understanding of "theme" in language arts, for example, may be different from the approach selected to teach argumentative writing. Teachers who seek to foster higher-level thinking and problem-solving skills in children are also aware that the same methods do not work for all children. Children learn best when the methods implemented acknowledge their individual approaches to learning. Fostering meaningful learning, or teaching for understanding, implies a sensitivity to the varied ways children learn and represent what they know.

The Work Sampling System Portfolio is a powerful tool that can help you understand what is involved in making possible meaningful learning in children. Although the connections between learning, curriculum, and assessment lie at the heart of teaching, students of teaching often lose sight of these important connections. They are more concerned with the *how* of teaching—the techniques and methods—than they are with the *what* and *why* of teaching. What are you teaching and why? And, how is that related to what you want your students to learn?

As prospective teachers, you come to teacher education programs seeking to learn how to teach. This is an important goal, but one that cannot be divorced from understanding what it is you will teach and your purposes for doing so. Fostering meaningful learning in children implies having a clear conception of each of these issues as well as an understanding of how they are connected. A first step in helping you understand this relationship is to develop an awareness of the different "kinds" of learning expected of children and how these differences are both directed by and captured in what children are asked to do. The following three assignments are designed to foster an awareness of the connections between learning, curriculum, and assessment and how those connections provide a foundation for fostering higher-level thinking and problem-solving skills in children.

Exercise 3.1   Connecting Teaching, Learning, and Assessment (In-Class Assignment)

Background

One of the many challenges for teachers is learning to think clearly about their goals and objectives for children. What do you want children to learn? It is important to consider this question when you plan instruction so that you do not miss opportunities for learning and teaching. The nature of your goals for children will influence your expectations for their learning and the activities you plan to support that learning.

Purposes

- To help you reflect on instructional goals and objectives

- To begin to consider the implications of these goals and objectives for the design of learning opportunities

Steps

1. In your small group, select a learning goal from the list of those you identified during your class discussion. If one has not been assigned to you, you will also need to select a grade level to use as a guide for your discussion about your goal.

2. With your specific goal and grade level in mind, discuss the following questions with the members of your group.

   - What kind of learning does that goal or objective imply: rote learning, memorization, application, or problem solving?

   - What prior knowledge or skills may be needed to lay the foundation for that achievement?

- What learning tasks or activities may foster the achievement of that goal or objective?

- How would a teacher know when children have achieved that goal or objective?

- What does this goal imply for what and how teachers teach?

3. Be prepared to share your discussion with the class.

Exercise 3.2   How Curriculum Materials Support Learning
(Out-of-Class Assignment)

Background

Students often look forward to the time when, as teachers with their own classrooms, they will be able to teach what and how they wish. In reality, much of your work will be guided by school or district curriculum materials or by national goals and standards. It is important that you learn to become effective users of such materials.

Purposes

- To help you become familiar with specific curriculum materials (texts, curriculum guidelines, and national standards and goals)

- To increase your sensitivity to the connections between teaching, learning, and curriculum

Steps

1. Before you leave class, make specific arrangements to get together with the other members of your small group.

2. When your small group meets, you will be reviewing and discussing the packet of materials you have been given. Use the following questions to guide your discussion.

   - What objectives and goals are represented in the guides or materials you are reviewing?

   - What kind of learning do those goals or objectives represent? Be specific.

   - What possible indicators of learning can you identify?

- What tasks and/or curriculum materials would support that learning?

- What are the implications for teaching?

3. Prepare a written summary of your discussion. Decide which points you want to share during your next class. As the small groups make their presentations, think about the following issues in preparation for a large-group discussion:

- Similarities and differences in the goals and objectives

- Factors that contribute to these similarities and differences

- General implications for learning

- General implications for teaching

Exercise 3.3   The Relationship between Instructional Tasks and Learning (Field Assignment)

Background

Learning how to observe and document children's learning opportunities is important for understanding the connections between teaching, learning, and curriculum. Being able to see these connections is a skill you will develop over time. This field assignment gives you the opportunity to practice that skill in an actual classroom.

Purposes

- To sharpen your observation skills

- To give you a chance to observe connections between teaching, learning, and curriculum in actual classrooms

- To have you reflect upon the information obtained

Steps

1. Contact the teacher in whose room you will be observing. Tell her that you want to make arrangements for several sequential observations of one child working in a particular subject area. Tell her that, after you have finished your observations, you would also like to talk to her about the child. If this is a teacher with whom you normally work in a practicum, make sure she understands that, for this assignment, you need to be able to just sit and observe.

2. Ask the teacher a few questions about her observation protocol. Does she want you to sit in a particular place during your observations? Be there at a certain time? Check in at the office first? Some teachers prefer that observers have no interactions with children; others don't care if you talk to children. What is this teacher's preference?

3. During your observations take comprehensive descriptive notes that record the following in as much detail as possible.

- What are the tasks and activities in which the child is involved?

- Does the teacher extend the child's ideas? How?

- What role does the teacher play in the child's activities?

- Are other children involved? How?

- What feedback does the child receive?

- Are tasks sequenced in some way? Describe.

- Does the teacher draw connections between the various tasks and activities in which the child is involved?

- How does the teacher assess the child's progress?

■ Is this information used? How?

Learning how to record observations takes practice. If you have not yet had much observational experience, use this as an opportunity to experiment with how to take notes.

4. After each observation take time to record your reflections about what you have seen. Your reflections should be guided by several questions:

   ■ How did learning goals appear to be reflected in the tasks and activities in which your child was involved?

   ■ How did the child represent the learning?

   ■ Are there other ways you can think of that might be used to represent that kind of learning?

   ■ What support was the child given? Describe.

   ■ What other factors appeared to contribute to the child's learning?

5. After you have completed your observations and reflections, talk to the classroom teacher. The purpose of this conversation or interview is to learn more about what you have observed in order to supplement your observations with the teacher's perspective. You will find it helpful to have your interview questions written out before you talk to the teacher. Include the following questions.

- What were the teacher's goals for the activities you observed?

- What kind of learning did the teacher want to foster?

- Why were the tasks appropriate for that child?

6. Next, integrate what you have learned from your conversation with the teacher into the rest of your work. Did the conversation help you understand things in a new or more complete way? Did it raise new questions for you?

7. Prepare to make a brief presentation to the class about your work. Make sure you address not only what you learned about the child's learning but also what you have learned about yourself as an observer.

C. *Illuminating Learning with Portfolios*

Portfolios encourage teachers to think about teaching and learning in differentiated ways. Examining a portfolio makes it clear that changes in the quality of a child's work over time can serve as evidence of learning. Similar items collected at different times illuminate a child's progress. In short, the use of portfolios and the work they include reflect teachers' understanding of the value and importance of ongoing, focused, and systematic documentation of children's learning.

As teachers begin to use portfolios to assess what and how children are learning, they begin to understand how different children may represent the same aspect of learning in very different ways. As they identify the various ways children represent what they know and how they know it, teachers are also forced to consider the implications of this variety in their instructional planning. How should instruction be planned so that all children are provided with equal opportunities to learn what is expected? How can learning opportunities be developed to address the variety of ways children in any one classroom learn? How can the understanding gained about individual children be used to structure learning opportunities that best meet the needs reflected in a classroom? Developing strategies to answer these questions should be an important goal of yours as you move through your teacher preparation, one that the Work Sampling System Portfolio can help you address.

The Work Sampling Portfolio is designed to document children's learning within seven domains (see Chapter 1): Personal and Social Development, Language and Literacy, Mathematical Thinking, Scientific Thinking, Social Studies, the Arts, and Physical Development. In combination with the *Guidelines*, working with the Portfolio will provide you with opportunities to consider carefully the different kinds of learning expected of children of different ages in different domains. Using this approach, you will become better able to identify those learning goals and objectives which foster meaningful learning and those which do not.

An examination of children's portfolio work prompts consideration of how children's skills, behaviors, and levels of thinking are revealed differently in different domains. For example, how a teacher and child decide to document specific aspects of learning in the domain of Scientific Thinking may be different from how they document work in the Language and Literacy domain. Additionally, how one child's learning is documented in a specific domain may be different from how their classmates' learning is represented and documented in that same domain. You may also see that the same example of work can serve as evidence for different aspects of learning in multiple domains.

Concrete representations of children's understanding and thinking provide information about how they have responded to instruction—what they have or have not learned. This information, in turn, guides further instruction. Thus, the work that children complete informs both instruction and assessment (Darling-Hammond, Ancess, & Falk, 1995). Use of the Work Sampling System Portfolio can help you understand these connections. As you develop these multiple understandings, the Work Sampling materials can also help foster a deeper understanding of curriculum. Examination of children's work in specific domains will help you understand how those domains can be organized for instructional purposes and which changes in children's work over time indicate authentic learning and progress in those domains. The following comments from a preservice teacher exemplify the understanding of performance and progress that you can begin to develop through examining children's work closely.

> Joe's journal entries are always excellent. He uses writing to convey meaning for a wide variety of purposes, and he writes very good fictional stories in his journal on a daily basis. One of my favorites was his story, "Halloween Ghost Tale." He has a strong grasp of the concepts of capitalization and punctuation, and uses these in his stories. All of his stories are sequential with understanding of beginning, middle, and end. Joe shows a lot of creativity and enthusiasm in this area of study. He does a good job using conventions of written language with increasing accuracy. He uses a lot of correct spelling in his journal entries. Joe has made a huge effort to increase his vocabulary this fall and the results are visible in his writing.

The following three assignments are designed to foster an understanding of how to learn from the work children produce.

Exercise 3.4   Comparing Achievement Tests and Performance Assessment (In-Class Assignment)

Background

Different types of assessments have different purposes and provide different information to students and teachers. You may be more familiar with achievement tests than you are with performance assessment methods such as portfolio collection. This assignment will give you the opportunity to examine a variety of achievement tests and several portfolio items, and to compare and contrast the types of information they provide to teachers.

Purposes

- To help you understand the difference between the information gained from typical achievement tests and that gained from portfolios

- To help you develop an appreciation for how performance assessment can help you know a child

Steps

1. Join your small group and begin by reviewing the achievement test you have been given. Critique it using the following.

   - What is the purpose of the test?

   - What information does the test provide about what the child knows?

   - What information does the test provide about how the child learns?

- How much flexibility does the child have in representing his knowledge?

- How can the information provided by the test be used to inform instruction?

2. Next, take a few minutes to familiarize yourself with the portfolio items. Use the questions listed in Step 1 to guide your critique of these materials.

3. Compare and contrast the two forms of assessment. Discuss the similarities and differences between the information a teacher obtains from the two sources.

4. Be prepared to summarize your findings for the class. In your summary you will want to address the purposes of the two forms of assessment, when and where each would be used most appropriately, and how each could be used to inform instruction.

Exercise 3.5   Learning about Learners through Portfolios (Out-of-Class Assignment)

Background

Well-structured portfolios have many benefits. Among these is the fact that portfolios help you assess what a child knows and can do. Equally important to you as a teacher will be the fact that portfolios also help you monitor a child's progress over time. This out-of-class assignment will help you understand how the systematic nature of Work Sampling System Portfolios is particularly suited to careful monitoring of children's progress over time.

Purpose

- To help you understand how portfolios allow teachers to see progress over time in very specific areas of learning

Steps

1. Before the next session of this class you will be expected to meet with the other members of your small group for the purpose of reviewing and critiquing a partial portfolio. That work session will probably be most helpful if each of you has some familiarity with the portfolio beforehand, so you may want to make arrangements for sharing it before you leave class today.

2. When you meet with your small group, discuss what the work samples suggest about the following:

   - The child's areas of strength

   - The areas in which the child needs additional work

- The child's progress in the different domains

- The learning opportunities provided for the child

3. Next, develop a clear summary statement describing what the child knows and can do, followed by an evaluation of the child's progress.

4. Now that you have some knowledge about this child's performance and progress, think about how you as a teacher could use that knowledge to plan for future instruction. Be as specific as you can.

5. Be prepared to share your discussion with the class.

Exercise 3.6   How Portfolios Work in Classrooms (Field Assignment)

Background

Learning to make connections between theory and practice is a critical part of learning to teach. This field assignment is designed to help you learn how some practicing teachers implement portfolio collection.

Purposes

- To help you understand how portfolios work in real classrooms

- To help you become aware of some of the issues teachers must address in order to use portfolios effectively

Steps

1. Select a partner for this interview assignment. Divide up the interviewing and note-taking tasks. For example, one of you may conduct the actual interview while the other takes notes, or if you both want some interviewing experience, you may decide to share the responsibility for both interviewing and note-taking.

2. Before you meet with the teacher, you will want to develop an interview protocol—a list of questions that will guide your conversation. As you do this, it is important to remember that your job is not to evaluate the teacher but to learn from her. Keeping that fact in mind will help you create and maintain a positive atmosphere during your interview. You will want to include the following questions in your protocol.

   - How long have you been using portfolios?

   - Why did you choose to use portfolios?

- How do you decide what materials to include in the portfolio?

- Are the children actively involved in the portfolio collection process? Can you tell me how that works?

- What other forms of assessment do you use? Do portfolios give you any information that differs from what you are able to capture through those other methods? Can you tell me more about that information and why it is important?

- Do you share the portfolio information with the child's family? If you do, how does the family seem to feel about the child's portfolio?

- What advice do you have for me about how to make portfolio collection work?

3. Come to the next class prepared to share the results of your interview.

D. *Identifying Areas of Learning and Core Items*

You can develop an understanding of meaningful learning by focusing your observations and work with children on the development of their higher-level thinking and problem-solving skills. These skills will be useful to children throughout their lives. Helping children develop these skills prepares them to be life-long learners who are able to think critically, solve problems, and take full advantage of the rapid changes in what we know. But these goals require a different approach to schooling and education than has often been the case in the past: they require an approach that is concerned with deep, conceptual learning and learning processes rather than with specific skills or narrow content (Blumenfeld, Marx, Patrick, & Krajcik, 1997).

Work with areas of learning and Core Items from the Work Sampling System Portfolio collection process will help to foster this understanding. In the first series of assignments in this chapter, you considered how general objectives for learning might differ, how different objectives might be reflected in children's work, and the implications this has for instruction. In the series of assignments that followed, you were asked to reflect on how portfolios help teachers learn from children's work. In this section we will discuss how working with areas of learning and the identification of Core Items can advance the idea of deep, conceptual learning. As you begin to consider the meaning of this view of learning, what it might look like, and how you would know when it was occurring, you will begin to appreciate the critical differences in learning prompted by the different kinds of work in which children are asked to engage. You will also develop a better understanding of how curriculum materials can be used to foster higher-level thinking and problem solving in all learners.

In the Work Sampling System, an area of learning is a strand of the curriculum (a part of a curriculum domain) that guides the collection of Core Items to be included in each child's portfolio (see Appendix E). Each domain encompasses many areas of learning. The Language and Literacy domain, for example, includes such areas of learning as "writing to communicate ideas" and "understanding and interpreting text," among many others. The domain of Mathematical Thinking includes such areas of learning as "using strategies to solve problems involving numbers" and "applying the concepts of patterns and relationships to solve mathematical problems." Identifying areas of learning, understanding their meaning, and learning how to document children's learning within them are important steps in helping you learn how to design meaningful learning opportunities for children.

In the Work Sampling System several key questions guide the selection of areas of learning:

- Is the area an important part of the curriculum?
- Is it specific enough that children can demonstrate progress within it over time?
- Is it relevant for all students?
- Does it reflect concepts or processes that are not dependent on particular content?

- Is it most effectively documented in a portfolio as opposed to some other way? Does it focus on understanding and performance rather than declarative knowledge?

The relevance of each of these questions to fostering and documenting meaningful learning is apparent. Meaningful learning reflects the integration of knowledge, skills, and developing understanding rather than the demonstration of a single or isolated skill. It enables children to apply several skills in context and demonstrate those skills as they represent their learning in a variety of ways. Teachers who foster meaningful learning address important parts of the curriculum—the "big ideas." In addition, they focus on abilities that develop over time and apply to all students of a particular age or grade, regardless of their place on the developmental continuum. When teachers emphasize meaningful learning and teach for understanding, they provide all students with opportunities to develop higher-level thinking and problem-solving skills as well as the basic skills. The concepts or processes that underlie or are fundamental to particular subject matter provide the foundation for deep conceptual learning and drive the curriculum. The focus is on how children think, approach tasks, and solve problems, not strictly on the solutions or answers they generate (Lampert, 1990). This type of performance is apparent in the work that children do and the documentation that accompanies that work. The following tasks will help you carefully consider these critical issues.

Exercise 3.7   Identifying Areas of Learning (In-Class Assignment)

Background

It is usually easier to think about measuring discrete skills than assessing higher-order thinking. Through this assignment you will see how the concept of areas of learning provides a framework for developing and organizing thoughtful, well-planned portfolios that document meaningful learning and higher-level skill development. The concept of areas of learning has an additional benefit for you as a prospective teacher. It can help you develop the habit of thinking beyond immediate outcomes and products and beginning to plan long-term projects.

Purposes

- To help you become familiar with the concept of areas of learning

- To assist you in understanding how areas of learning can be used to guide portfolio collection and to document meaningful learning systematically

Steps

1. In your small group take a few minutes to review the five criteria for effective areas of learning.

   - Is it an important part of the curriculum? Does it focus on understanding and performance rather than just factual knowledge?

   - Is it specific enough to show progress over time?

   - Is it relevant for all students?

- Does it reflect concepts or processes that are not dependent on particular content?

- Is it most effectively documented in a portfolio as contrasted to some other means?

2. Now, brainstorm several areas of learning for a different domain. Evaluate each against the five criteria for effective areas of learning. Keep careful notes of your work and questions.

3. Select one area of learning that meets all five criteria for effective areas of learning. Identify as many skills and concepts contained within this area of learning as possible.

4. Exchange your work with another small group so that you can critique each other's areas of learning and lists of skills and concepts. Address the following questions:

- Do you agree with the areas of learning the group selected? Why or why not?

- Can you think of additional skills and concepts that might be contained within those areas of learning?

Exercise 3.8   Identifying Core Items (In-Class Assignment)

Background

You are already familiar with areas of learning and understand that they refer to specific parts of a curriculum domain. You also know that areas of learning focus your attention on children's deeper understandings and higher-level thinking skills. This assignment will familiarize you with another Work Sampling System concept: Core Items. Core Items are representations of particular areas of learning within a domain.

This assignment begins a discussion of the learning opportunities that enable children to demonstrate proficiency in areas of learning and how those learning opportunities can be designed to allow for multiple ways for children to represent their learning.

Purposes

- To familiarize you with Core Items

- To help you begin to understand how to design learning opportunities related to areas of learning

- To help you begin to understand the multiple ways children's participation in learning activities can be represented

Steps

1. Before you begin the in-class part of this assignment, it is important to make sure that you have a working understanding both of the term *areas of learning* and of the criteria for developing them. If you think you are not quite clear about something related to this concept, clarify your understanding before you go on (see Appendix E, p. 153). You will find that a clear understanding of areas of learning will make it easier to proceed with your work on Core Items.

2. Take fifteen minutes to complete the Core Item Collection Worksheet for the area of learning that you have been assigned. In the left column, describe classroom activities that will engage students in this area of learning.

3. On the right side, list the products that children create as they engage in the learning activities listed on the left. Focus on products that can become part of a child's portfolio. Provide careful detail about various ways to represent learning. It is very likely that children can represent their learning from each activity in several different ways, depending on each child's preferred means of expression.

4. Exchange your worksheet with another student and critique each other's work. Take a few minutes to reflect on the entire process and be ready to share your reflections with the class.

Exercise 3.9   Meaningful Learning (Field Assignment)

Background

One of the difficulties faced by prospective teachers is the translation of college- or university-based classroom work to the world of practice that is found in elementary classrooms. This activity will help you consider how meaningful learning can be fostered in actual classroom settings by giving you a chance to analyze the organization and activities within one classroom.

Purpose

- To help you consider how classroom activities and routines can be structured to support meaningful learning

Steps

1. Before you begin, take a few minutes to reflect on your understanding of the concepts of areas of learning and Core Items. In order to complete this assignment, you will need to spend several hours observing in an elementary school classroom. During this observation you will concentrate on observing activities children are engaged in within the domain assigned to you.

2. During your observation, take careful and specific notes about what the children are doing. Unless you are a highly experienced observer, you will probably find it difficult to reflect on the meaning of what you are seeing while you are actually in the classroom, so save that reflection until after your have completed your observation.

3. Try to find the time to sit down and complete your observation report as soon after you complete your observation as possible. Many people find there is so much to see during group observations that they take notes that are clear only to themselves. You will need to revise your notes to make them clear to others.

4. Next, reflect on what you observed. In your reflection consider the following:

- What kind of learning (e.g., basic skills, problem solving, or higher-level thinking) do the activities you observed seem to represent?

- What area of learning does each activity seem to represent?

- Do these areas of learning meet the five criteria for effective areas of learning? Why or why not?

- What are some activities that could be used to support higher-level thinking in the area of learning? (Remember that you are observing for only a few hours, so there will be much that you do not see during your visit.)

- If you did not think the activity you observed promoted higher-order thinking, how might the structure and organization of the classroom be changed to facilitate this?

- What are some other ways that teachers could elicit concrete evidence of higher-level learning?

5. Be prepared to share your findings with the class at the next session.

E. *Documenting Learning*

Many factors influence how teachers make sense of children's work:

- their professional knowledge,
- their goals for learning,
- their understanding of the curriculum,
- the learning opportunities they provide for children, and
- the approach that each child takes to learning.

The items in a portfolio are visible representations of children's learning and progress. As a teacher reviews the child's work, she translates it into both a description of the child's learning and an assessment of that child. The understanding that is an outcome of that description and assessment process contributes, as well, to a potential revision of the teacher's own instruction and curriculum. If children are not learning what a teacher wants them to learn in the way she wants them to learn it, it is her professional responsibility to teach it in a different, more effective way, or to rethink the goals selected or the curriculum chosen. To make this process work, it is essential that teachers document the contexts in which children's portfolio items are created as well as the processes informing those artifacts.

As beginning students of teaching you have had few opportunities to reflect on the connections among educational goals, learning opportunities provided to children, how specific children represent that learning, and implications for the future instruction of each learner. As prospective teachers your focus on the "how" of teaching often comes ahead of consideration of what a teacher chooses to teach and why she chooses to teach it. Your work with the portfolio component of the Work Sampling System in your teacher preparation program provides rich opportunities for you to begin to reflect on the following:

- What do I want children to learn?
- Why do I want children to learn this?
- What learning opportunities will enable them to do so?
- How might I structure learning opportunities to best encourage this learning?
- What are the various ways children might represent this learning?
- How will these opportunities broaden my understanding of the learners in my classroom?
- How will they help the learners progress and develop?

These understandings can be developed by examining, reflecting on, and writing commentary about specific examples of children's work. You will quickly see that in order to communicate to others what a piece of work represents about a child's learning, you first need to understand how that work represents the goals established for learning and the opportunities provided for the child. Writing commentary about portfolio items encourages this understanding. Practice in writing commentary also prepares you for the synthesis and integration that are the foundation for narrative reports. Narrative reports of children's learning are being used more and more in school systems around the country. Even when narrative reports are not used, an important aspect of teachers' work is communicating to parents the information that would be included in such a report. Learning to write commentary about individual pieces of work lays the foundation for learning how to summarize multiple observations and examples of work that tell a teacher about a child's learning in a particular domain and across domains. The following three assignments are designed to foster your understanding and reflection on what children's work indicates about their learning and, *in turn the learning opportunities provided for children.*

Exercise 3.10   Children's Work as a Reflection of Learning (In-Class Assignment)

Background

Children's work tells us a great deal about children's learning. Multiple examples of similar work from different time periods enable us to learn about children's progress. Successful portfolio collection is dependent on a teacher's ability to interpret children's work and to annotate work with comments that enhance our understanding of the work.

Purposes

- To allow you to analyze children's work in order to learn about their performance and progress

- To help you identify the information children's work gives about the teacher's goals and future instructional plans

- To encourage you to reflect on the documentation that should be included with children's work

Steps

1. With a small group of students, review the piece of work that you have been given. As you look at the work, reflect upon the following:

   - What does the work seem to tell you about the child?

   - How has the child represented her learning?

   - What do you think the child was trying to accomplish?

- How successful was the child at what she was trying to accomplish?

- What do you think the teacher's learning goals for the child might have been?

2. Next, think about the other information you may need in order to have an accurate sense of the child as a learner (e.g., the time of year, child's prior knowledge, conditions supporting the work, relation to planned curriculum).

3. List the documentation (e.g., specific details, notes, commentary) you could collect in order to elaborate on the information each sample or work gives you about a learner.

4. Share your discussion with the large group. Contribute your ideas to the composite list of information teachers should keep to document children's work.

Exercise 3.11   Learning to Write Commentary (Out-of-Class Assignment)

Background

Understanding children through their work involves more than knowing which samples of work to collect and how to collect them. It also requires that teachers know the type of documentation that needs to accompany the work if it is to enhance teachers' understanding of children and to guide instruction.

Purposes

- To help you learn how to document children's work

- To help you learn how to write commentary on children's work

Steps

1. You and a partner will be assigned a sample of a child's work from a Work Sampling System Portfolio Review Materials Set or some other example of children's work.

2. Before the next class, review the work and add documentation to it.

3. Write a summary to go along with the work based on your answers to the following:

   - What does the work seem to tell you about the child?

   - How has the child represented her learning?

- What do you think the child was trying to accomplish?

- How successful was the child at what she was trying to accomplish?

- What do you think the teacher's learning goals for the child might have been?

4. Remember that you are looking at and thinking about a very limited amount of the child's work. What else would you need to know to write a more accurate summary about this piece of work? For example, what about the time of year when the work was done, prior assessment data on the child, the contextual conditions supporting the work, or where the work fits in relation to the planned curriculum?

5. Bring a copy of your written summary to share with your partner who reviewed the same material. Begin by reading your partner's summary. How are the two commentaries alike? How are they different? Why? After reviewing your partner's work, would you make any changes to your own?

6. Share your work, documentation, summary, and reflections with the class.

Exercise 3.12   Learning about Work from the Perspective of the Learner (Field Assignment)

Background

An important aspect of interpreting each child's work is understanding that child from his own perspective. One way to gain this understanding is to involve the child as an active participant in the portfolio collection process. Moreover, involving children in self-evaluation is an important way to nurture their motivation for learning. Throughout this term-long assignment you will come to know one child through that child's work and words.

Purposes

- To help you understand children's learning from the child's perspective

- To help you learn how to make the child an active participant in the portfolio collection process

Steps

1. This is a complex assignment, one which requires repeated observation and interaction with a specific child. It is important that both the child's classroom teacher and the child's parent or guardian understand what you will be doing and why you will be doing it. Your professor has drafted a letter explaining the project to them. If these letters have not already been distributed you may be asked to help do that.

2. Once teachers, classrooms, children, and parents have been identified, you will need to get permission to observe and review the school work of one child throughout the term. Some of you will find getting permission to be a relatively easy process; some of you will find it more difficult. Among the issues you need to consider are these:

   - Who should you talk to at the school? The principal? The teacher? Both?

- Does the school or district have a permission form for you to use, or will you need to bring one of your own?

- Do you need to get permission from the child's family? Will you use the same form or a different one? How will you get in touch with the family and what will you say?

- What about the child? Should you obtain the child's permission?

- How will you describe this project to the school and family?

3. Collect copies of the signed written permission forms. These will need to be reviewed by your professor before you begin this project.

4. Develop a written plan. Make sure that your plan addresses the following:

- Plans for formal observations. How often will you observe the child? Will you observe at different times and in different domains or are you more interested in learning about one particular domain?

- Plans for gathering and commenting upon the child's work. Does the child's teacher already have procedures in place for collecting children's work? If she does, will you be using that collection, or will you be gathering additional samples or work? How often will you do that?

- Plans for involving the child in the process throughout the term. Will you talk to the child each time you are in the room or only at certain times? What form will the child's commentary take? Does the child have the skills needed to supplement verbal commentary with written commentary?

Include a specific timeline. Remember that your reflections about this process of involving children in assessing their own work is as important as what you learn about the child, so make sure you address this in your plan.

5. If you have not yet had much direct classroom experience with children, you may want some preparation. Let your professor know if you feel you need more than the assistance you have received in class. Mock interviews, role plays, selected readings, or a chance to see modeled conversations with children may all help you feel more confident.

6. Once your plan has been reviewed and revised, you are ready to begin your formal observations, collection of work, and meetings or conversations with the child. Talk to the classroom teacher to arrange a time to begin.

7. You will be submitting progress reports to your professor. It is important to work on this assignment throughout the semester, rather than waiting until the end.

8. Toward the end of the term you should arrange to meet with the child. You want to understand what the child thinks about the learning he has been engaged in throughout the semester. As you think about that conversation, consider how you might get the child to answer the following:

- What have you learned this year?

- What activities helped you to learn that?

- What is your best work? Favorite work? Why?

- What do you want to learn next?

- What would help you learn that?

- How has your portfolio helped you to learn this year?

9. Write a reflection paper on the experience of "learning from the perspective of the learner" that addresses these points:

- What are the similarities and differences between your interpretation of the child's work and progress and the child's interpretation?

- What is the relationship between the teacher's objectives and the child's interpretation of what she has learned?

- How have your interactions with the child added to your understanding of the interactive nature of teaching and learning?

- What have you learned about the child that would help you work with that child and other children in the future?

- How would you structure future meetings of this kind?

- If you were to do this project again, what would you do the same? What would you do differently?

10. You will be expected to submit a final report on this project by the end of the term. That report will be submitted in the form of a loose-leaf notebook, sections of which will include:

- a description of your project,

- copies of your written observations,

- notes describing your conversations with the child,

- samples of the child's work, including commentary on that work, and

- final reflections and summary.

F. Summary

Developing the ability to foster meaningful learning is one of the most complex aspects of learning how to teach. It encompasses much of teaching's ambiguity and requires deep understandings of teaching, learning, curriculum, and assessment. In this chapter we used the Work Sampling System Portfolio to help you begin to develop these understandings. A first step in fostering meaningful learning is to consider the goals for learning and the connections between teaching, learning, and assessment. Teachers that hope to foster meaningful learning must provide opportunities that enable children to engage in meaningful tasks. The objectives and goals a teacher establishes, the curriculum materials used, and the instructional tasks developed may all support or hinder meaningful learning. Becoming sensitive to these issues is a necessary condition for learning how to develop meaningful learning opportunities for children. The Work Sampling System Portfolio provides insight into how to accomplish this goal.

Use of the Work Sampling Portfolio as a way to structure your examination of the practice of teaching is intended to foster the understanding that learning about learners in a way that informs instruction requires observation, documentation, and assessment of children's work in an ongoing, systematic manner. You learned what is required to make sense of children's work and how portfolios can be used to provide a deep and broad understanding of children as learners, children's learning and development over time, and how learning occurs in multiple domains and is represented in multiple ways. As a form of performance assessment, the Work Sampling System Portfolio draws attention to the limited understanding provided by traditional forms of assessment. It prompts reflection on all of these issues, and thus provides a foundation for a richer understanding of teaching.

The Work Sampling System areas of learning and Core Items concepts, in particular, facilitate this deeper understanding. Considering how to identify areas of learning and Core Items illuminates how the tasks teachers ask children to engage in may or may not foster higher-level thinking and problem-solving skills. Critical examination of children's work allows you to reflect on how instruction can and should be designed to support and document important aspects of learning—aspects of learning that are relevant to all students and that illuminate progress over time. You begin to understand that teaching and learning are interactive processes, each informing the other through the process of assessment. Documentation of learning is a key step in coming to understand the interactions between teaching and learning. The Work Sampling System Portfolio offers rich opportunities for you to learn how to make sense of children's work and how to develop documentation that supports meaningful learning and assessment. This, in turn, guides an understanding of the interconnections among teaching, learning, curriculum, and assessment.

References

Barton, J., & Collins, A. (1993). Portfolios in teacher education. *Journal of Teacher Education, 44*(3), 200–210.

Blumenfeld, P. C., Marx, R. W., Patrick, H., & Krajcik, J. (1997). Teaching for understanding. In B. J. Biddle, T. L. Good, & I. F. Goodson (Eds.), *The international handbook of teachers and teaching* (pp. 819–878). Dordrecht, The Netherlands: Kluwer.

Bransford, J. D., Brown, A. L., & Cocking, R. R. (Eds.) (1999). *How people learn: Brain, mind, experience, and school.* Washington, DC: National Academy Press.

Cohen, D. K., McLaughlin, M. W., & Talbert, J. E. (1993). *Teaching for understanding: Challenges for policy and practice.* San Francisco: Jossey-Bass.

Darling-Hammond, L., Ancess, J., & Falk, B. (1995). *Authentic assessment in action: Studies of schools and students at work.* New York: Teachers College Press.

Grace, C., & Shores, E. (1991). *The portfolio and its use: Developmentally appropriate assessment of young children.* Little Rock, AK: Southern Association of Children Under Six.

Lampert, M. (1990). When the problem is not the question and the solution is not the answer: Mathematical knowing and teaching. *American Educational Research Journal, 27*(1), 29–63.

Tharp, R., & Gallimore, R. (1988). *Rousing minds to life: Teaching, learning, and schooling in social context.* Cambridge: Cambridge University Press.

Assessing Learning

In this chapter we discuss the importance of developing an understanding of the role that assessment plays in teachers' work. We use the Work Sampling System Summary Report to help you learn how to analyze, integrate, and summarize the observations and documentation of learning that are an on-going part of a teacher's responsibilities. The Summary Report serves a number of functions: as a structure for helping you understand the steps involved in evaluating children's learning, as a model and framework for learning how to write narratives that accurately portray student learning, as a medium for communicating with children's families, and as a tool for refining your understanding of the important ways that performance assessment serves teaching and instruction. The assignments with this chapter are designed to take advantage of all of these functions. They are intended to help you, as prospective teachers, develop not only skill in assessing learning but also the reflective habits of mind that are an essential characteristic of effective and responsible educators.

A. Introduction

Assessment involves two complementary processes: documentation and evaluation. A teacher's observations and documentation of student learning are necessary conditions for the assessment of student learning. However, they are not sufficient. Observation and documentation reveal what the child can do; evaluation indicates how successfully children have learned what was expected of them. All teachers are required to make some judgment about children's learning. These judgments may be related to external standards or to more subjective criteria. In Work Sampling, for example, the *Guidelines* represent national standards, while the Portfolio is designed to capture classroom expectations and objectives that reflect a teacher's professional experience, knowledge of child development, and the local curriculum. Regardless of the approach taken, evaluation implies judgment of children's performance and progress.

In the Work Sampling System the Summary Report is the means by which a teacher transforms the information integrated from observations, documentation, and portfolios into an evaluation of performance and progress that can be communicated to families and to others in the school district. (See Appendix F for a copy and examples of a Summary Report.) The Summary Report requires teachers to reflect on all the evidence they have collected so they can make reasoned and informed evaluative decisions. This is a formidable task. Summary Reports can be used to learn how to accomplish this task effectively and responsibly by helping you distinguish between performance and progress, helping you learn how to write narrative reports (learn how to summarize multiple observations and examples of work that tell a teacher about a child's learning in a particular subject area and across subject areas), and helping you communicate with families. In addition, discussions of the Summary Report with your peers and teachers provide opportunities to reflect on the political and ethical issues raised by various approaches to assessing and reporting student progress and performance.

The Summary Report can be used to help you learn how to make distinctions between performance and progress by prompting such questions as: What does it mean to say a child is progressing? Which evidence is necessary to make a distinction between performance and progress? What standards should be applied? What do different levels of mastery look like in the classroom? How do different children demonstrate and represent their level of mastery? How might progress in different domains be identified?

The Summary Report can also be used to forge a link between assessment and instruction. As you learn to write narrative reports that illustrate children's performance and progress, you learn that although instructional decisions are prompted by many factors, ultimately the choices teachers make should be driven by the instructional needs of each learner. The content being taught, the goals and objectives embedded within the curriculum, the standards guiding different disciplinary domains, and the teacher's knowledge of her subject and of pedagogy all influence the choices made. Work with Summary Reports encourages you to consider what any narrative report should contain, what evidence best provides the basis for assessment decisions, how a teacher determines when sufficient information is collected, and how the narrative report illuminates what a teacher can do to help children accomplish those goals.

Summary Reports are also intended to provide a foundation for reporting to parents. Communicating with families entails new learning for you as students of teaching. Meaningfully communicating the complex nature of each child's learning has become increasingly difficult as the diversity in the race, primary language, ethnicity, and socioeconomic background of nearly every classroom group has increased (Gordon, 1992; Nieto, 1992). These family differences are important aspects of who each child is as an individual and a learner. Understanding the richness in that diversity is a necessary condition not only for understanding children as learners, but also for communicating effectively with the families of children. Work Sampling's focus on the individual learner can begin to sensitize you to the differing ways children learn and help you understand the influence of race, primary language, ethnicity, and socioeconomic background on each child as a learner.

Finally, work with Summary Reports can encourage you to consider the political and ethical issues raised by different systems for assessing and reporting student progress and performance. Learning how to use Summary Reports provides you with the opportunity to reflect on what the goals of assessment are and should be, on whether systems of assessment are fair to all children, and on the best ways to ensure that assessment of performance and progress is fair and unbiased.

Exercise 4.1   Reflecting on Evaluation

Background

The word *evaluation* is heavily value laden and inspires strong feelings. Your own experience of being evaluated will influence how you think about assessment. Reflecting on possible barriers to effective evaluation will help you to overcome those barriers in your future practice.

Purposes

- To give you an opportunity to reflect on the meaning that evaluation has for you

- To help you understand how your experience of being evaluated influences how you think about assessment

- To encourage you to consider possible barriers to effective evaluation, barriers you will need to overcome in your future practice

Steps

1. Write a reflection paper on what evaluation means to you. In this paper discuss:

   - A positive and a negative experience you had while being evaluated

   - An instance when your ability in some area was accurately assessed and another instance in which an evaluation of you was highly inaccurate

   - The factors that you think contributed to these positive and negative experiences

   - The role you believe assessment plays in teaching

2. At the next class meeting, be prepared to share your reflections with other students in a small group.

B. *Evaluating Performance*

Reflecting on children's performance is an ongoing aspect of teachers' work. Making judgments about the adequacy of performance and progress implies an understanding of what can be expected of children at different grades in different subject areas. Knowing whether a third-grade student is developing his ability to think mathematically, for example, is grounded in an understanding of the typical mathematics curriculum in the third grade; of the thinking skills, problem-solving abilities, and behaviors that reflect mathematical thinking; and of what can be expected of typical third-grade students. Coupled with this knowledge, however, is knowledge of the particular child being assessed. What can be expected of one student may be very different from what can be expected of another child. Rather than holding each child to an absolute standard according to which all children are expected to demonstrate performance in exactly the same way, assessment that guides instruction focuses on the performance of each child, her strengths and weaknesses in different domains, and the particular ways she demonstrates her learning (Meisels, 1996a).

Learning how to evaluate performance in this way requires that you first distinguish between performance and progress and understand the multiple ways progress in different domains may be demonstrated and captured. It also requires an understanding of the kind of evidence needed to make those distinctions, how standards can be used to inform decisions, and what different levels of mastery look like in the classroom.

The first step is learning how to distinguish between *performance* and *progress*. Focusing on the temporal dimension in each may help you keep this distinction in mind in your own practice. The evaluation of performance is an examination of a child's current capabilities in comparison to a particular standard. In contrast, the evaluation of progress is an examination of what a child can now do as compared with what the child did in the past. Evaluation of performance is concerned with a single point in time. Evaluation of progress is concerned with more than one point in time. Because experienced teachers often concentrate on progress rather than on performance, it is essential that you understand that although some children may never meet particular expectations (performance), all children grow and develop (progress). Evaluation is not the end of a process but the beginning of a new cycle of teaching; because a child is not able to do something at one point in time does not mean she will not be able to do so in the future. Developing an understanding of the relationship between assessment and teaching will help you develop an awareness of the responsibilities educators have to respond instructionally to assessment information. Maintaining a distinction between performance and progress is an aspect of that responsibility.

As prospective teachers, you must also come to understand the role that standards play in effective evaluation and assessment. A child's performance may be measured against externally imposed standards (e.g., Goals 2000), curriculum-embedded standards (e.g., NCTM standards), or a teacher's own goals and objectives (e.g., fostering children's prosocial behavior). You must understand these distinctions. If you are not clear about the standards children are being measured against, you will neither be able to design learning opportunities that will help them meet these standards, nor will you be able to assess children's progress adequately. As prospective teachers you must also become sensitive to what can be expected of learners of a given age in different domains, regardless of the standards children are being measured against (Darling-Hammond, 1994). Working with the Work Sampling System can help you develop these understandings. The *Omnibus Guidelines* provide clear expectations and examples of children's accomplishments in different domains and at different ages. The Portfolio illuminates the different ways children represent their learning. The Summary Report provides opportunities to synthesize a teacher's knowledge about learners and address how they have progressed. The Summary Report also emphasizes the need to integrate information and documentation collected from multiple sources over time before making evaluative decisions about learners. A first step in learning how to conduct meaningful assessment is understanding what these multiple sources are and how they interact.

Exercise 4.2   Structuring Assessment and Evaluating Learning (In-Class Assignment)

Background

The Summary Report provides a structure that can help you learn about assessment decisions and how assessment information becomes integrated into a coherent picture of a learner. The different parts of the Summary Report contain elements that are necessary for any assessment approach.

Purposes

- To familiarize you with the various components of the Summary Report

- To help you understand how assessment information is integrated into a coherent picture of a learner

- To help you look at assessment information from the perspectives of the teacher, the family, and the learner

Steps

1. In a small group discuss the blank Summary Report form you have been given. (See Appendix F.) Use the following questions as your guide:

   - What is being assessed (domains and components)?

   - How it is being assessed (ratings/observations/documentation)?

   - What different standards are being used?

   - How are the ratings supported (comments)?

- Is the difference between performance and progress clear?

2. Now look at the completed Summary Report you have been given and discuss the following:

- What information does the Report communicate about the child's current level of performance?

- What can you learn about the child's progress from the ratings?

- Do the comments support the ratings?

- Does the Report address strengths and areas of teacher concern?

- In what ways does the Report address plans or goals for the future?

- What is your reaction to the Report in terms of specificity, amount of detail, and descriptiveness?

- What is your reaction to the overall tone of the Summary Report? Would you describe it as positive, respectful, negative, critical, hopeful, vague, or appreciative?

- If you were the child's parent and you were reading this report, would you think that the teacher knows your child? If so, what are the clues that lead you to think this? If not, what else might be included?

3. Summarize the characteristics of an effective assessment of learning from

- The teacher's perspective: Does it communicate the learning goals established? Does it communicate how instruction supported the child's pursuit of those goals? Does it communicate how the information will be used to inform future instruction?

- The family's perspective: Does it capture a complete picture of the child? Does it communicate the learning opportunities provided to the child? Does it communicate what the child has learned?

- The learner's perspective: Does it reflect what the child knows and can do? Does it reflect how the child demonstrates learning? Does it communicate progress? Does it communicate what the child will experience?

4. Finally, discuss how all these elements are related to effective assessment decisions.

Exercise 4.3   A Critical Review of a Summary Report (Out-of-Class Assignment)

Background

In this assignment you are given an opportunity to review and reflect on a completed Summary Report. Learning to make assessment decisions and recognizing when those decisions are adequately supported by evidence are difficult tasks. The Summary Report is a tool that can help you begin to understand how to accomplish both of these tasks.

Purposes

- To help you reflect critically on a completed Summary Report

- To give you practice in learning what to look for when reviewing assessment decisions

- To help you reflect upon possible barriers to meaningful and unbiased evaluations

Steps

1. Join a group of students who share your interest in a particular grade level. A copy of a completed Summary Report for a child in that grade will be given to each of you.

2. Before our next class, each of you should write a critical review of the Report. In your review, address the following:

   - What information does the report communicate about the child's current level of performance?

   - What can you learn about the child's progress from the ratings?

- Do the comments support the ratings?

- Does the Report address strengths and areas of concern?

- In what ways does the Report address plans or goals for the future?

- What is your reaction to the Report in terms of specificity, amount of detail, and description?

- What is your reaction to the overall tone of the Summary Report?

- If you were the child's parent and you were reading this report, would you feel that the teacher knows your child? If so, what are the clues? If not, what else might be included?

3. During the next class you will be asked to share your review with the other students who examined the same Summary Report and to reflect on the similarities and differences among the reviews. You will also be asked to discuss the characteristics of effective and ineffective assessments of learning, possible barriers to effective evaluations, and ways to overcome those barriers.

Exercise 4.4   Capturing Learning (Field Assignment)

Background

Summarizing learning is a process which requires much practice and reflection. This assignment will provide you with an opportunity to practice writing narratives or summaries of children's learning. It is a beginning step in learning how to conduct effective assessments and write good reports.

Purposes

- To give you practice in summarizing one aspect of learning for a specific child

- To give you practice in writing summary narratives with supporting documentation

- To help you reflect on your summary of learning in a critical manner

Steps

1. Before our next class you will need to complete an observation of one child for a specified period of time and for a particular area of learning or unit of instruction. For example, you may observe one child for two weeks as the child's class keeps track of daily weather changes. During the observation, document the child's learning with ongoing notes and, if possible, supplement your observations with examples of the child's work.

2. Use both your written notes and the child's work to form the basis for a written summary describing that child as a learner. Draw from previous assignments with Summary Reports when structuring your summary.

3. Include a section critiquing your summary and reflecting on the process of developing it. What made it difficult to write? What do you think you did well?

4. During our next class you will be asked to share your summary with a partner and to critique each other's work using the following guiding questions.

  ■ What information does the summary communicate about the child's current level of performance?

  ■ Does the summary identify both strengths and areas of concern?

  ■ What is your reaction to the summary? Is it sufficiently specific, detailed, and descriptive?

  ■ Discuss the overall tone of the summary: Is it positive, respectful, negative, critical, hopeful, vague, or appreciative?

  ■ If you were reading this summary as the child's family member, would you feel that the teacher knows your child? If so, why? If not, what is missing?

5. Discuss how you would use this information in a Summary Report and what other information you would need to complete the assessment within the domain represented by the area of learning.

6. Discuss and develop a plan describing how you would strengthen and expand future written summaries.

C. *Writing Narratives*

Good narratives of student learning provide a coherent picture of a child. The stories they tell are supported and elaborated on by observations and collections of children's work over a period of time; these stories must have a strong evidentiary base. In addition, good narratives are clearly written and contain specific vignettes that capture each child's individuality. As is apparent in the following reflection, this preservice teacher is developing the ability to tell the story of the child as learner.

> Karen may have told you that last month we had a special speaker for Children's Book Week. Dr. Smith is an author of children's books and a professor. Due to a communication problem, I was unsure of the time of his talk, as well as of the content he would deliver. This kind of uncertainty is commonly unsettling for third graders, but Karen managed the transition and adjusted her behavior to the new situation with ease. She listened attentively to Dr. Smith and asked appropriate questions.

Narrative reports communicate the ways in which a teacher fosters meaningful learning for children. Learning how to write narratives of children's progress helps you develop as a professional in several ways. The narratives provide opportunities to reflect on the teaching and learning process. They enable you to test concretely what it means to develop a basis of evidence for assessment decisions. They also foster reflection by encouraging practice in integration and synthesis.

Good narratives comprise several elements (Cortazzi, 1993). The following observations by a preservice teacher illuminate how narratives can address a child's strengths and areas of teacher concern.

> Greg is beginning to use strategies to create invented spellings in his writing. He has made progress using initial consonants and letter–sound correspondence. He occasionally whispers the sounds of words aloud while reading and writing, but prefers to figure out the spellings inside his head. Greg has started to attempt to use closer approximations of conventional spellings as well. He prefers to copy conventional spellings than create invented spellings for words when he writes. He is also making good progress using some of the conventional spellings of words he sees often in print such as *and, the, like,* and *but.* I have observed that Greg is making wonderful progress in his spelling development.
>
> Greg seems to have a very secure self-concept and does not have trouble choosing someone with whom to work and play. He is a very dedicated student and is always among the first students to settle down and complete his work. Greg has demonstrated a wonderful amount of self-control both in and out of the classroom, and I hope that he continues to do so over the course of the year. I would like to see him become more flexible in his approach to new activities, even if that means leaving a task unfinished for a short time when interrupted. His flexibility should improve with increased experience during the day.

Effective narratives convey information essential to understanding the child as a learner and depicting the child's individuality. As you learn to write narrative reports, you will build on what you have been learning about the observation and documentation of learning. You will learn how to describe and interpret children's work and how to substantiate judgments. Writing narratives will also help you learn to avoid educational jargon, to maintain a positive tone, and to develop suggestions for how families can work with children at home.

The assignments you do next are intended to provide you with opportunities to learn how to develop coherent, integrated, and meaningful assessments of children's learning by addressing the following:

- What should a narrative report contain and why?
- How do I provide evidence to support my claims?
- How do I determine if the information is meaningful for its intended audience?

Exercise 4.5   Capturing Student Learning with Narrative Reports (In-Class Assignment)

Background

Narrative reports capture children's learning through multiple sources of information that result from ongoing observation and documentation. Learning to write narratives is an important skill to develop. This assignment will help you focus on specific aspects of narrative reports and how they relate to a coherent, meaningful picture of a learner.

Purposes

- To help you learn the specifics of what to include in a narrative report

- To help you reflect on how to develop coherent, integrated, and meaningful narratives of children's learning

Steps

1. Work in small groups to discuss the details of writing narrative reports. For your discussion, focus on one domain and grade level. During your discussion consider the following elements of narrative reports that effectively summarize children's learning.

2. What descriptive information will best capture the child's learning?

   - A list of the activities the child engaged in?

   - The times when those activities occurred?

- The specific behavior(s) you observed?

- How the child represented her learning?

- The evidence you used to support your descriptions?

3. When answering the questions in Step 2, also consider the proper amount of detail to include and the appropriate level of specificity.

4. What does that information mean in relation to

- the child's areas of strength,

- the child's areas of weakness, and

- the implications for future learning?

5. What evaluations of the child's learning does the information lead to, and how should those evaluations be presented? Does it evaluate

- performance?

- progress?

6. Who is the audience for the report, and how does the information address that audience?

- Families

- Learners

- Other educators

Exercise 4.6   Beginning to Write Narratives (Out-of-Class Assignment)

Background

Synthesizing and summarizing multiple sources of information in order to create meaningful Summary Reports about learners is a skill that takes time and practice to develop. In this assignment you will use a child's portfolio to write a narrative report on a learner.

Purposes

- To give you an opportunity to write a narrative report based on work included in a child's portfolio

- To have you reflect on and discuss your narrative report with other students

Steps

1. Using the framework developed in Exercise 4.5 and the child's portfolio that you have been given, write a short narrative report describing the child.

2. At the next class meeting, be prepared to share your narrative with the other students who examined the same portfolio.

3. Compare narratives, noting similarities and differences.

4. Reflect on the process and on what you would do differently in the future.

Exercise 4.7   Writing Narratives (Field Assignment)

Background

This assignment will give you practice in bringing together all the pieces needed to write an effective narrative report. By writing a narrative report you will have the opportunity to put into practice what you have been learning, discussing, and observing this semester.

Purposes

- To give you a chance to conduct an ongoing extended observation of one child's learning in specific domains

- To give you practice documenting those observations

- To allow you to complete a narrative report on the child's learning

Steps

1. Conduct an ongoing extended observation of one child in one or two specified domains. Document your observations. Be sure to include samples of the child's work in your documentation.

2. Write a complete narrative report on the child in the specified domains. Write the evaluation as if you will be sending it home to the child's family. Include sufficient information for the family to understand why you are evaluating their child as you are, and include specific examples of the growth you have seen over the course of the semester.

3. Make recommendations that are specific to the child you have been observing. Indicate the child's areas of strength in each domain you have chosen to observe, the areas the child still needs to work on, and what you would do to encourage further growth. In making these recommendations be very clear about how you are substantiating your recommendations. For example, what have you learned in other courses that has influenced your recommendations? Cite specific references whenever you can to make explicit connections between theory and practice.

4. Reflect on the process you went through to complete the narrative. How did you learn about the child? What made you feel confident about your work? What made you feel unsure about your work? What would you do differently? What would you repeat? Why?

5. Critique your report. Address the strengths and weaknesses of your report, how well you think you know the child as a learner, and how well you communicated that knowledge through your written narrative.

D. Communicating with Families

As we discussed in the previous section, written narratives describing children's progress can help teachers both better understand the development and learning of individual children and reflect upon that learning as evidence of the success of their own practice. Writing narratives offers the chance to reflect on the learning opportunities children have been provided, on how those opportunities have been supported and documented, and on how that documentation informs future instruction. Children's learning, however, is influenced by contexts far wider than those encompassed by the teacher's own practice. Families, neighbors, communities, and culture influence the child and what the teacher discovers about the child. This information must also become part of the process of reflecting on the child's learning and planning for instruction. The comments below were made by a preservice teacher observing a third-grader who was having a difficult time developing relationships with other children. The comments capture the preservice teacher's reflections.

This is Charlie's first year in this school. He moved here from a neighborhood where he had many friends (according to his mother), and from a school where he apparently was at the "top of the class." Not many of Charlie's classmates live in his new neighborhood and, because the neighborhood is "rough," Charlie's mother does not allow him to play in the neighborhood as he might have done where he used to live. The teacher has spoken to Charlie's mother, so Ms. Brown is aware of the problems Charlie is having at school this year and has noticed changes in Charlie's behavior at home, as well.

Communication with families is an aspect of teaching that often receives little emphasis in teacher education programs and, as novice teachers, you may view this task as simply a matter of passing along your knowledge to the child's family. As the concept of a transmission model of educating children has fallen out of favor, so too has the transmission model of working with families been proven to be ineffective. Today we speak of the need for a partnership between families and schools (Lewis, 1996). For many reasons, however, we find this partnership difficult to create. Increasingly, teachers come from cultures that differ from those of many of the children with whom they work, they live outside of the communities in which they work, and they have fewer opportunities to become familiar and comfortable with the habits of thinking and behavior of the children in their classrooms. Higher numbers of single-parent families and women who work outside the home add the barrier of insufficient time to those already enumerated. Communication between families and teachers can become fragile indeed.

For many of you there may be two additional constraints: age and inexperience. The thought of suggesting to families what to do can be rather unsettling for someone still dependent on his or her own family of origin. You may worry about how to say a child is not doing well, or how to communicate with families who speak a language other than your own. As is true with most of us when we begin to acquire a new skill, you may also worry about the numbers of people who will be directing your lives as teachers and see families as just one more member of this group of stakeholders, this group of people who will tell you what to do.

The feeling of uncertainty created by all of these factors may be exhibited as uncertainty, disinterest, or even reluctance to work cooperatively with families. However, you need to avail yourself of every opportunity to learn to begin to see families not as opponents but as partners in and contributors to the child's learning. The use of the Work Sampling Summary Report form and process can play an important role in helping you to develop and understand families as partners who can support children's learning.

Exercise 4.8   Reflecting on the Process through Role Play (In-Class Assignment)

Background

Learning how to communicate assessment information to parents in a way that is meaningful and supportive requires extensive practice. This assignment is designed to help you explore some of the confounding factors you may face as you communicate with parents about their children.

Purposes

- To provide you with an opportunity to practice communicating with parents

- To help you learn to deal with potential factors that might confound communication between teachers and families

Steps

1. Review a completed Summary Report and Portfolio packet in preparation for conducting a role play with a peer about how you would communicate the information contained in those documents to the child's family. Outline the child's strengths and areas of difficulty as detailed by the Summary Report and illustrated by the work.

2. Take the time to reflect critically on any characteristics of the child that may have influenced her learning and learning opportunities. Among the factors you may want to consider are gender, SES, race, ethnicity, and primary language.

3. Reflect on the ways the child's background differs from your own, and how this may influence your understanding of the child.

4. Develop a plan for how you would present this information to the child's family.

5. Use the plan you develop to conduct a role play with your partner.

6. Critique each other's presentations, addressing all the factors listed above, including how each of you can improve in the future. Be prepared to share with the class any difficulties you encountered and ways you might change your approach in the future.

Exercise 4.9   From the Families' Perspective (Out-of-Class Assignment)

Background

Communication between families and teachers is a two-way process. In order to develop a sound understanding of the dynamics of communicating with families, you will need to be aware of the perspectives of as many of the participants in the process as possible. This assignment gives you an opportunity to interview a parent and to discuss assessment issues from the family's perspective.

Purposes

- To make you more aware of the perspectives of parents

- To help you understand some of the dynamics involved in communicating with families

Steps

1. Arrange to interview a parent. If possible, interview a parent who is different from you in some way. You may, for example, decide to interview a parent who is different from you by virtue of race, ethnicity, or SES.

2. During the interview, ask the parent to address such questions as:

   - What assessment or evaluation methods are used at his child's school? Does the child receive letter grades, or ratings such as Satisfactory/Unsatisfactory? Are results of standardized tests such as state tests and the Iowa Tests of Basic Skills shared with the parents?

   - What have the assessment methods at the child's school taught the parent about his child?

- What have they taught the parent about the education the child is receiving?

- How well do those assessment methods portray this child as an individual?

- How could the assessment process be improved?

3. Write up your interview and be prepared to share your findings with the rest of the class.

4. Working with your peers, generate a list of ways in which communication with parents about their child's performance and learning in school can be improved.

Exercise 4.10   From the Teacher's and Child's Perspective (Field Assignment)

Background

Teachers and children also are participants in the circle of communication on assessment issues. Their perspectives on the assessment process need to be explored if you are to master the dynamics of effective communication between schools and families. In this assignment you will have the opportunity to interview both a teacher and a child about the assessment process.

Purposes

- To help you become aware of the perspectives of teachers and children on assessment issues

- To help you explore the dynamics involved in effective communication with teachers and children

Steps

1. Interview a teacher. Questions to be asked include:

   - Does the teacher provide opportunities for parent and student input into the assessment process? For example, does the teacher seek out information from the parents, either formally or informally? Does the teacher gather input from students?

   - How does the teacher provide opportunities for both parent and student input into the assessment process? How does the teacher make use of this information?

   - Why did the teacher select this particular approach to gaining parent and student input? What are the reasons for the choices she makes?

2. Interview a child as well. Ask the child:

■ How does your teacher evaluate your learning in the classroom? Do you receive letter grades, ratings, etc.? Does your teacher write comments on your work? Do you read the comments?

■ What have you learned about yourself from being assessed? What would you like to learn from the assessment?

■ What would you like to tell the teacher about the assessment process? What would you change about the process?

■ Is there any other information about the assessment process that you would like to know?

3. Write up both interviews and be prepared to share your findings in class.

E.   Instructional Assessment as an Aspect of Responsible Teaching

Assessment can provide teachers with a clear view of children's skills, knowledge, and behaviors, as well as an appreciation of their strengths, and an understanding of their areas of difficulty. A teacher's decisions and actions transform this information into instructional strategies, educational plans, and dynamic learning experiences. Without a sensitive and meaningful approach to assessment, however, this transformation is often unrealized.

The form of assessment with which most teachers are familiar is norm-referenced testing. Norm-referenced tests are used to compare children's performances to sets of norms or to the average scores of other children of the same age. Hence, the meaning of a child's score on a test of this type is relative to the rest of that group of children, not to a curriculum or to any other set of developmental criteria. Communication between assessment and instruction is not very effective in a norm-referenced context. That is, the test neither adequately informs future instruction nor does instruction influence what should be assessed and how it should be assessed.

Instructional performance assessment, in contrast, represents a significantly different approach to assessment. Performance assessment methods allow children to demonstrate their knowledge, skills, dispositions, and other aspects of development and expression through solving problems, acting on their environments, interacting with individuals in their own settings, experimenting, talking, moving, and so on. These assessments are formative: they provide information that can be used both to change the process of instruction and to keep track of children's progress and accomplishments. They are ongoing, with information collected about the child and her setting on a structured but continuing basis. The information obtained is used both for instruction and for the process of assessment. Because these kinds of assessments are continuous, they can also be used to monitor a child's progress longitudinally instead of only summarizing that progress on annual or semi-annual occasions.

Instructional assessments require multiple sources of information and multiple observations of the same or related phenomena before conclusions can be drawn, something this preservice teacher is learning—.

> Two mornings a week for three hours each day, I have been able to observe Greg's growth and social, personal, and educational development over the course of the semester. Through my observations, I was able to collect a considerable amount of data about how he interacts with the other children. I have watched him interact with his seat mates both after journal time and during independent seat work as well. During calendar and story time each morning, I had the chance to watch Greg's behavior and responses. Thus, I was able to see Greg both as a participant and as a bystander in these activities. During recess or morning break, I had the opportunity to observe Greg from afar as he played. My role in the classroom gave me many chances to work with Greg one-on-one as well. Occasionally I worked alone with Greg reading a book, completing writing activities, participating in a variety of math games, and during various assessment tasks I was given by the cooperating teacher. I was also

able to observe and interact with Greg during a cooperative learning activity and while he completed his independent seat work. When I was not otherwise occupied with my responsibilities in the classroom, I observed Greg in both my free time as well as in his.

Instructional performance assessments rely on extensive sampling of behavior in order to derive meaningful conclusions about individual children. Moreover, they are highly sensitive to differences in the quality of children's performances. Two children may have highly comparable skills, but they may demonstrate these skills in very different ways. Performance assessments provide systematic information about qualitative differences between children and change within a single child when that child is evaluated over time. Unlike other types of assessments, performance assessment transforms the historical model that separated assessment and instruction from each other into one that fuses assessment and instruction into a common set of procedures. Performance assessment is based on the recognition that information obtained from the educational context is the most useful information possible for enhancing a child's achievement—information that accounts for the complexity of development, the impact of environment, the influence of parental figures, and the role of context (Meisels, 1996b; Meisels & Atkins-Burnett, 2000).

Work Sampling can be used to help you develop this kind of understanding. Learning to conduct focused, systematic, unbiased observations of students, developing a rich understanding of areas of learning and the student work that captures that learning, and learning to write narrative reports synthesizing and integrating what you have learned, all will help you come to realize the importance of the connection between assessment and instruction. You will learn, as well, that the methods of assessment predetermine in significant ways the learning opportunities with which children are provided. All methods of assessment are not equally fair to all children; the best way to assure fairness is to use methods of assessment that provide the evidence that helps teachers foster meaningful learning in each child (Meisels, Dorfman, & Steele, 1994). The following assignments illuminate the power of instructional performance assessment.

Exercise 4.11   Learning about Learners through Assessment (In-Class Assignment)

Background

This assignment is designed to draw your attention to some of the specific differences between norm-referenced tests, standardized tests, and performance assessment measures.

Purposes

- To have you review and compare different forms of assessment

- To help you discuss what teachers can learn about children from each type of assessment

Steps

1. In a small group, discuss the different forms of assessment. Focus on the following questions:

   - What is the purpose of each form of assessment? How do the purposes differ?

   - What information is gained from each? How does the information from each differ?

   Be sure to include examples of the following kinds of assessments:

   - Teacher-made tests

   - Standardized tests

- Performance assessments

2. Review a multiple-choice test, a worksheet, a unit test included with curriculum materials, and examples of a child's work that your small group has been given.

   - What does each of these tell you about the child as a learner?

   - How can each be used to inform future instruction?

   - How would you summarize what the child knows based on the information presented?

3. Share the results of your small-group discussion with the class.

4. Join the members of your small group again. This time compare standardized and performance methods of assessment, focusing on a specific domain and grade level. Discuss the following:

   - What does each method tell you about the children as learners?

   - What does each method tell you about what children know and how they have learned it?

- What does each method tell you about the learning opportunities with which children have been provided?

- What does each method tell you about the learning opportunities children need in order to progress?

- How can the information gained from each measure be used to inform instruction?

- How does each form of assessment represent the individuality of each child as a learner?

5. Share your discussion with the rest of the class.

Exercise 4.12   Biases in Assessment Methods (Out-of-Class Assignment)

Background

What role does bias play in different forms of assessment? All assessment methods do not evaluate all children in an equally fair and unbiased way. The most fair assessment for any child is that which provides information that the teacher is able to use to foster meaningful learning for the child.

Purposes

■ To help you explore the role that bias plays in different forms of assessment

■ To allow you to consider assessment methods from the perspective of the needs of different children

Steps

1. You have been provided with copies of both a norm-referenced test and a performance-based assessment.

2. Select a particular domain (e.g., mathematics or reading) to use as you review each form of assessment and, with that domain in mind, review both the norm-referenced test and the performance-based assessment from the perspective of

   ■ a student with a reading disability,

   ■ a student whose primary language is not English, and

   ■ a student who comes from a lower socio-economic background.

3. Reflect on the advantages and disadvantages of each form of assessment for the learners described in Step 2.

- How relevant is the form of assessment to the child's background or experience?

- Does it allow the child to represent learning in a variety of ways?

- Does it provide the child with opportunities to compensate for any learning problems that he may have?

4. Write up your review for the next class. Be prepared to share your reflections, and to discuss how and why some forms of assessment may be biased against some learners.

Exercise 4.13   Assessment in Classrooms (Field Assignment)

Background

This assignment requires that you conduct a series of observations on how children are assessed in several classrooms. Assessment outcomes are most useful when they inform instruction by providing teachers with meaningful educational information about the children in their classrooms. The value in new forms of assessment becomes more relevant when they are viewed in juxtaposition to the outcomes of more traditional forms of assessment. Looking into real classrooms will help you better understand the ethical and political consequences of testing.

Purposes

- To have you observe classrooms that are using a variety of assessment methods

- To have you reflect on the relationship between assessment outcomes and the instructional needs of children

- To have you continue to reflect on the ethical and political consequences of testing

Steps

1. Conduct a series of observations in several classrooms. Over a number of classroom sessions, observe how students are assessed both formally and informally including looking at the following:

   - The role that assessment plays in instruction

   - The learning opportunities provided for children based on their assessment

   - The feedback provided to children that is generated from assessment

2. Reflect on the possible consequences of the methods of assessment for children's learning in the classrooms you observed.

 ■ Does instruction differ for individual children based on different assessment outcomes?

 ■ Does instruction differ for groups of learners based on different assessment outcomes?

 ■ Is the curriculum informed by assessment?

3. Would performance-based measures of assessment make a difference in any of the classrooms you visited? Why or why not?

4. Write a report based on your observations addressing the issues discussed in Steps 1–3. Be prepared to share the results of your observations and reflections in class. During class, help generate ideas for how you will assess the children you teach when you become a teacher.

F. Summary

Developing the ability to assess student learning is an essential aspect of learning how to teach. Assessment is multidimensional and complex and provides information crucial to practice. What children understand and are able to do provides the basis for further instruction. Learning how to make judgments about children's learning helps you better understand the connections between teaching, learning, and curriculum. In this chapter we discussed how to develop an understanding of the role that assessment plays in teachers' work. We addressed how the Work Sampling System Summary Report can be used to learn how the integration and summarization of a teacher's observations and documentation of learning provide the substance for assessment and to help ensure developmentally appropriate practice. The Summary Report provides a structure to help you develop a professional understanding of the steps involved in evaluating children's learning, a model and framework for learning how to write narratives that capture student learning, and a tool for communicating with families.

The Summary Report is a tool to help you learn how assessment is structured and how to draw distinctions between performance and progress. Attending to what is being assessed, how it is being assessed, and the standards used as points of comparison are all essential aspects of effective assessment. The use of the Summary Report helps develop an understanding of how important it is for teachers to substantiate their judgments of student progress and how those judgments inform future instruction.

The Summary Report also serves as a model and framework for learning how to write narratives that portray student learning. Well-written narratives clearly communicate what a child can do and have implications for future learning and instruction. Meaningful narratives, drawing from multiple sources of information and forms of documentation, build a coherent, integrated picture of each learner, representing the child's strengths and weaknesses, performance and progress, and individuality.

Learning how to communicate with families is another important aspect of learning how to teach. Children coming to school these days are increasingly diverse, while the makeup of the teaching force is becoming more homogeneous. The Summary Report can help you learn how to share evaluation information with families and can help enrich your understanding of the children with whom you will work. Reflection on what you, as prospective teachers, do and do not know about children and their families is prompted by consideration of the multiple factors and personal characteristics that influence how children learn. In addition, finding opportunities to talk with parents, teachers, and children about assessment and your perspectives on how the methods used do or do not capture children in all their complexity can expand the limited understanding you bring to your preparation program. The richer the understanding you are able to develop, the better prepared you will be to meet the educational needs of a rapidly changing student population.

The Summary Report can also provide a focus for your consideration of the strengths and weaknesses of various forms of assessment. It prompts consideration of the political and ethical ramifications of the assessment choices teachers make, including who benefits and who does not: How do the assessment choices teachers make influence the learning opportunities with which different children are provided, and what are the long-term implications of this? Using the Work Sampling System can help you begin to consider the full complexity of the assessment choices teachers make and how closely assessment is linked to fair and unbiased teaching, curriculum choices, and meaningful learning opportunities.

References

Cortazzi, M. (1993). *Narrative analysis.* London: The Falmer Press.

Darling-Hammond, L. (1996). Performance-based assessment and educational equity. *Harvard Educational Review, 64* (1), 5–30.

Gordon, E. W. (1992). *Implications of diversity in human characteristics for authentic assessment.* CSE Technical Report 341. Los Angeles: National Center for Research on Evaluation, Standards, and Student Testing (CRESST).

Lewis, N. (1996). *Families and schools: An essential partnership.* Tallahasse, FL: Southeastern Regional Vision for Education.

Meisels, S. J. (1996a). Performance in context: Assessing children's achievement at the outset of school. In A. Sameroff & M. Haith (Eds.), *Reason and responsibility: The passage through childhood* (pp. 407–431). Chicago: University of Chicago Press.

Meisels, S. J. (1996b). Charting the continuum of assessment and intervention. In S. J. Meisels & E. Fenichel (Eds.). *New visions for the developmental assessment of infants and young children* (pp. 27–52). Washington, DC: ZERO TO THREE: The National Center for Infants, Toddlers, and Families.

Meisels, S. J., & Atkins-Burnett, S. (2000). The elements of early childhood assessment. In J. P. Shonkoff & S. J. Meisels (Eds.). *The handbook of early childhood* (2d edition, pp. 231–257). New York: Cambridge University Press.

Meisels, S. J., Dorfman, A., & Steele, D. (1994). Equity and excellence in group-administered and performance-based assessments. In M. Nettles (Ed.), *Equity in educational assessment and testing* (pp. 195–211). Boston: Kluwer Academic Publishers.

Nieto, S. (1992). *Affirming diversity: The sociopolitical context of multicultural education.* New York: Longman.

Appendixes

Glossary of Terms

Area of Learning—a strand of a curriculum domain that guides the collection of Core Items.

As Expected (performance)—a performance rating on the Summary Report that indicates that the child's performance as seen in the Checklist or Portfolio meets or exceeds age- or grade-level expectations.

As Expected (progress)—a progress rating on the Summary Report that indicates that the child has grown appropriately according to the teacher's professional judgment and knowledge of child development.

Checklist—*see* **Developmental Checklist**.

Checklist Ratings—*see* **In Process, Not Yet, Proficient**.

Collection Period—a duration of time during which data are collected in an ongoing manner in order to make an evaluation. Work Sampling has three collection periods: fall, winter, and spring.

Component—*see* **Functional Component**.

Core Items—Representation of a particular area of learning within a domain; collected from five domains three times a year and designed to display both the quality of children's work and their progress in domain-related knowledge and skills.

Curriculum-embedded—an assessment that uses students' actual performance in the regular classroom routine as the "data" for evaluation.

Criterion-referenced—an assessment that evaluates a student's work with reference to specific criteria rather than with reference to other students' work.

Developmental Checklist—a list of performance indicators for each grade level that are organized by curriculum domains and are used to collect, organize, and record teachers' observations.

Developmental Guidelines—a book that describes age- or grade-level expectations for the performance indicators; contains a rationale and examples for each indicator.

Domain—a broad area of the curriculum.

Examples—descriptions of ways that children demonstrate what they know and can do related to each performance indicator in the *Developmental Guidelines*.

Functional Component—a subset of a domain comprised of several performance indicators.

Guidelines—*see* **Developmental Guidelines**.

Indicator—*see* **Performance Indicator**.

Individualized Items—Portfolio items that capture the child's unique interests and experiences, and reflect learning that integrates many domains of the curriculum.

In Process—a Checklist rating that indicates that the skill or knowledge represented by a performance indicator is intermittent or emergent, and is not demonstrated consistently.

Needs Development—a performance rating on the Summary Report that indicates that the child's current performance does not meet age- or grade-level expectations.

Not Yet—a Checklist rating that indicates that a child cannot demonstrate the skill or knowledge represented by a performance indicator.

Omnibus Guidelines—two volumes (P3–3, K–5) that each display six years of *Developmental Guidelines* on facing pages, arranged to show year-to-year progress.

Other Than Expected—a progress rating on the Summary Report that indicates that a child's progress is either above or below teacher expectations.

Performance—refers to the level of a student's behavior, skills, and accomplishments at a particular point in time.

Performance Assessment—refers to assessment methods that rely on students demonstrating their knowledge or skills in applied situations.

Performance Indicator—a skill, behavior, attitude, or accomplishment that is evaluated in the classroom.

Proficient a Checklist rating that indicates that the skill or knowledge represented by a performance indicator is demonstrated consistently, and is firmly within the child's repertoire.

Progress—growth over time.

Portfolio—purposeful collection of children's work.

Rationale—a brief explanation of an indicator that includes reasonable age- or grade-level expectations.

Summary Report—a report completed three times during the school year that integrates information from the Developmental Checklist and Portfolio with teachers' knowledge of child development in order to evaluate a student's performance and progress.

Summary Report Performance Ratings—*see* **As Expected (performance), Needs Development**.

Summary Report Progress Ratings—*see* **As Expected (progress), Other Than Expected**.

The Work Sampling System

The Work Sampling System helps teachers document and assess children's skills, knowledge, behavior, and accomplishments by observing, recording, and evaluating a wide variety of classroom activities and areas of learning on multiple occasions. Designed for use in preschool through the fifth grade, Work Sampling is a comprehensive way to monitor children's social, emotional, physical, and academic progress. It is an authentic performance assessment that consists of three complementary elements: (1) teacher's observations informed by the *Developmental Guidelines* and recorded on Developmental Checklists; (2) regular collection of children's work in Portfolios; and (3) teacher summaries of this information on Summary Reports each fall, winter, and spring.

These elements are all classroom-focused and instructionally relevant, reflecting the objectives of the classroom teacher. Instead of providing a mere snapshot of narrow academic skills at a single point in time, the elements of the System work together to create an ongoing evaluation process designed to improve both the student's learning and the teacher's instructional practices.

One of Work Sampling's strengths is its systematic structure. This structure allows teachers to collect extensive information from multiple sources and to use this information to evaluate what children know and can do. In its reliance on observing, collecting, and summarizing, Work Sampling organizes the assessment process so that it is both comprehensive in scope and manageable for teachers and students. A description of the mechanisms for observing, collecting, and summarizing follows.

The *Developmental Guidelines* provide a framework for observation. They give teachers a set of observational criteria that are based on national standards and current knowledge of child development. The *Guidelines* set forth developmentally appropriate expectations for children at each age or grade level. In using the *Guidelines* as the basis for their professional judgments, teachers in different settings can make decisions about children's behavior, knowledge, and accomplishments using identical criteria. Teachers record their observations on the Developmental Checklists.

Portfolios are purposeful collections of children's work that illustrate children's efforts, progress, and achievements. These collections are intended to display the individual nature and quality of children's work and their progress over time. Work Sampling advocates a structured approach to portfolio collection through the collection of two types of work samples: Core Items and Individualized Items. Core Items are designed to show growth over time by representing the same area of learning on three separate occasions during the school year. Individualized Items are designed to portray the unique characteristics of the child and to reflect work that integrates many domains of the curriculum. Child and teacher are both involved in the design, selection, and evaluation of portfolios.

A Summary Report is completed three times a year. Teachers combine information from the Developmental Checklists and the Portfolio with their own knowledge of child development to make evaluative decisions about student performance and progress. They summarize their knowledge of the child as they make ratings and write brief comments describing the student's strengths and their own areas of concern. Summary Reports take the place of conventional report cards.

The Work Sampling System addresses seven categories, or domains, of classroom learning and experience. These seven domains are as follows:

    I. Personal and Social Development. This domain emphasizes emotional and social competence. A teacher learns about children's emotional development—their sense of responsibility to themselves and others, how they feel about themselves and view themselves as learners—through ongoing observation, conversations with other children, and information from family members. Teachers learn about children's social competence by interacting with them, by observing their interactions with other adults and peers, and by watching how they make decisions and solve social problems.

    II. Language and Literacy. This domain organizes the language and literacy skills needed to understand and convey meaning into five components: Listening, Speaking, Reading, Writing, and Research. Students acquire proficiency in this domain through extensive experience with language, print, and literature in a variety of contexts. Over time students learn to construct meaning, make connections to their own lives, and gradually begin to critically analyze and interpret what they hear, observe, and read. They begin to communicate effectively both orally and in writing for different audiences and purposes.

    III. Mathematical Thinking. The focus in this domain is on children's approaches to mathematical thinking and problem solving. Emphasis is placed on how students acquire and use strategies to perceive, understand, and solve mathematical problems. Mathematics is about patterns and relationships, and about seeking multiple solutions to problems. In this domain, the content of mathematics (concepts and procedures) is stressed, but the larger context of understanding and application (knowing and doing) is also of great importance.

IV. **Scientific Thinking.** This domain addresses central areas of scientific investigation: inquiry skills and the physical, life, and earth sciences. The process of scientific investigation is emphasized throughout because process skills are embedded in—and fundamental to—all science instruction and content. The domain's focus is on how children actively investigate through observing, recording, describing, questioning, forming explanations, and drawing conclusions.

V. **Social Studies.** Encompassing history, economics, citizenship, and geography, the domain of social studies emphasizes social and cultural understanding. Children acquire this understanding through personal experiences and from the experiences of others. As children study present day and historical topics, they learn about human interdependence and the relationships between people and their environment. Throughout social studies, children use a variety of skills, including conducting research, using oral and visual sources, solving problems systematically, and making informed decisions using the democratic process.

VI. **The Arts.** The emphasis in this domain is on children's engagement with the arts (dance, drama, music, and fine arts), both actively and receptively, rather than mastery of skills and techniques related to particular artistic media. The components address two ideas: how children use the arts to express, represent, and integrate their experiences, and how children develop an understanding and appreciation for the arts. It focuses on how opportunities to use and appreciate the arts enable children to demonstrate what they know, expand their thinking, and make connections between the arts, culture, history, and other domains.

VII. **Physical Development and Health.** The emphasis in this domain is on physical development as an integral part of children's well-being and educational growth. The components address gross motor skills, fine motor skills, and personal health and safety. A principal focus in gross motor skill is on children's ability to move in ways that demonstrate control, balance, and coordination. Fine motor skills are equally important in laying the groundwork for artistic expression, handwriting, and self-care skills. The third component addresses children's growing ability to understand and manage their personal health and safety.

Work Sampling not only provides the teacher with clear criteria for evaluation but also incorporates the teacher's expertise and judgment. An evaluation system that does not dictate curriculum or instructional methods, it is designed for use with diverse groups of children in a variety of settings and is closely aligned to state and national curriculum standards. The Work

Sampling System is a flexible framework for assessment that helps teachers structure their assessments systematically and that encourages teachers to devise techniques best suited to their styles, their students, and their contexts. Extensive research about Work Sampling's psychometric properties is available.

The three elements of the Work Sampling System form an integrated whole and draw upon teachers' perceptions of students while informing, expanding, and structuring their perceptions. The System allows teachers to assess children's development and accomplishments—rather than their test-taking skills—in meaningful, curriculum-based activities. It enables them to recognize and nurture children's unique learning styles, instead of rigidly classifying children as high or low achievers based on simplistic assessments. It enables families to become actively involved in the assessment process. And by objectively documenting what children learn and how teachers teach, Work Sampling provides for meaningful evaluation and genuine accountability. The Work Sampling System's comprehensive design also provides a structure to foster the professional development of prospective teachers.

Approaches to Classroom Observation

Teachers conduct classroom observations in at least three different situations: when they are in the midst of the classroom action, by stepping out of the action, and by reflecting after the fact. Some teachers will use one form of observation more frequently than another, depending on what fits their classroom, their style, and the planned activities for any particular day.

Participating in the Action

Most observation occurs during ongoing activities when teachers are talking with students, facilitating group activities, or circulating among students who are working independently. In fact, it is a misconception that effective observation can only be accomplished by stepping back—carefully watching only one child and writing down everything that that child is doing. Teachers observe as they are teaching. Observation in this way provides teachers with a wealth of information, which is often difficult to remember because so much is taking place simultaneously.

The missing element when teachers observe while participating in the action is documentation. It is essential for teachers to establish realistic expectations about how much is possible to record "in the action" and to understand that observations recorded "in the action" will not be as rich or detailed as those taken "out of the action." Nevertheless, they provide a valuable source of evidence about children's learning.

Stepping out of the Action

Teachers can also observe by stepping out of the action and focusing exclusively on observing and documenting those observations. It is important to recognize that stepping out of the action usually occurs for very brief periods of time. In busy classrooms, teachers might only step out of the action once or twice a day, a few days each week. Because classrooms are complex and busy places, it is not expected that teachers will remain out of the action for long periods of time.

Reflecting on the Action after the Fact

Some teachers observe informally throughout the day and then take time after students leave for lunch or at the end of the day to take notes about what they observed that day. Recording observations several hours after they happened means that this form of observation is more likely to be influenced by opinion, so it is critical that teachers write only what they saw, not their interpretations. Some strategies teachers have used include the following:

- reviewing a class list and jotting a note about each child,
- recalling something about five children each day, and
- recalling one activity and writing all you can remember about students' performances during that activity.

Observational Methods

Brief Notes

Brief notes, also known as jottings, are quick notes that serve as a reminder of observed events.

Anecdotal Records

These are narrative accounts that describe a particular event factually. Usually they are created by first jotting down brief notes and adding details later. They provide rich, detailed information.

Running Records

Running records are detailed narrative accounts of behavior recorded in a sequential manner, just as it happens. They include all behavior that occurs within a given time frame. Like anecdotal notes, they provide rich information, but require the teacher to step out of the action.

Rating Scales

Rating scales are tools that indicate the degree to which a student possesses a certain skill.

Matrices

Matrices provide a way to write brief notes or make a simple rating of a skill or set of skills for a few children or for the entire class. Names of students are listed on the left-hand side of a page. Specific skills, concepts, or behaviors are listed across the top.

Tallies

To use a tally, the teacher watches a student or a group of students for a predetermined amount of time and counts all instances of a particular behavior.

Time Samplings

Time samplings are used to record the frequency of a behavior's occurrence over time. A teacher might check on a child every five minutes to note the different activities the child engages in during Choice Time.

Example of a Brief Note

This third-grade teacher, circulating among six different groups of children as they worked on reading projects, observed from the midst of the action. Her plan was to record brief notes about three children. She had mailing labels attached to a clip board. The questions in the back of her mind were, "How are these children functioning in the context of their reading groups?" and "Does the work they do in the reading group demonstrate comprehension of the text?" Here is her brief note.

> 8-year-old—reading group
> 1/15/9x R.L.
> skit of Mrs. BEF w/TW, GK, ES
> org. grp into roles
> R acted w/express—phys + verb
> repeated reminders to grp that seq. of skit follow story

Transcription: Third graders are at work in small groups reading novels. R.L. is working with three other students on a skit about the book *From the Mixed Up Files of Mrs. Basil E. Frankweiler.* He organized the group so that they each had a role. When acting, he used physical and verbal expression. He persisted in getting the rest of the group to keep the action of the skit consistent with the sequence of the story.

Example of an Anecdotal Record

This anecdotal record was written by a preschool teacher who had stepped out of the action to observe Dwight cooking. She recorded her anecdote on an index card (which was attached to a file folder). Her descriptive narrative captures the details of Dwight's interest, physical actions, and language. Very often teachers write anecdotal recordings using shorthand and then transcribe them. This anecdotal record or a quote from it could be used in a conference or on a Summary Report to convey the quality of Dwight's language.

> Anecdotal Record (4-year-old, cooking)
> 11/5/9x Dwight

Dwight is at the table cooking cranberries with Brian and Nancy (assistant). He is seated on his chair leaning over the table with his elbows on his chin. His lips are pursed and he is frowning a little bit. He watches. B stirs with the wooden spoon. D says, "I see smoke." Sugar, water, and cranberries are heating on the hot plate. N says, "This is steam, Dwight. Not smoke." D says, giggling, "Brian that steam's getting on your face." He sits up on his knees, his two hands on the table. "I want to stir now. I want steam in my face." He takes the spoon and begins to stir, putting his face near the pot.

Example of a Matrix

The first-grade teacher using this matrix observes from the midst of the action over the course of a week. She has planned a series of measurement activities for her students in which they will work with partners to measure different parts of their bodies. They can use materials of their choice, such as Unifix cubes, or cuisenaire rods, as non-standard units of measure.

To prepare for her observations, she uses a matrix on which she has recorded the names of her students and specific skills related to the activity. The skills she will look for include counting and lining up the measuring unit from the baseline, estimating length with non-standard units, accurately measuring the recording, and describing the process.

She has created a code for herself that consists of a "✔" when she clearly sees the skill, an "x" when the child has not yet developed the skill, and a "~" when the child is grappling with or just beginning to develop the skill. In addition to using the code, she occasionally records a note. For example, she observed Louis on Monday. He was trying to measure Melvin's leg using Unifix cubes. The teacher noticed that he couldn't line them up and that he kept losing count. She suggested that he use orange cuisenaire rods instead. She made this suggestion because they are longer and therefore he would have fewer to count. He was able to line the rods up from the baseline, but needed help counting and recording the number.

The teacher also observed Tina, noting that she did not have an understanding of the use of a consistent unit of measure. Tina tried measuring Jessica using a combination of rods and cubes. Observing this, the teacher reviewed the concept of consistent units and suggested Tina use only Unifix cubes. Tina then lined up the cubes from the baseline, counted accurately when the length was short (e.g., hand, arm) but had difficulty as lengths increased (e.g., leg, whole body).

Knowing that children would be working on variations of this activity all week, the teacher tried to observe a few children each day. This illustration shows the information she had after two days of observing.

This method of documentation doesn't capture all the details of each observation. However, it is practical because it enables the teacher to document information quickly. The combination of her code and additional notes helps her to recall details when she reviews this information to plan the next lesson or complete the Checklist.

FIGURE C.1. *Measurement Activity: Use Manipulatives to Measure Body Parts. Date: 4/22–26.*

✓ yes ✗ no ~ emergent **Child**	Count and line up from baseline	Estimate length with non-standard units	Accurately measures and records	Describes process
Ben	✓ w/unifix	~	✓	✓
Dimitri	w/rods ~ misses base			
Elena		~	~	
Ellis				
Jessica				
Kevin	✓ w/unit blocks	✓	✓	✓ verbal ~ written
Kiesha	✓ worked with Larissa	~	✓	~
Larissa	✓ yellow rods	✓	✓	✓+ verbal & written
Louis	✗ w/unifix ~ suggested orange rods	✗	~ w/rods	
Melvin				
Ramon	✓ w/unit blocks	✓ arm, leg ~ full body	✓	✓
Tina	~ consistent unit ~ picked unifix	✗	✓	✓

Documentation Tools

Mailing Labels

Attach a strip of mailing labels to a clipboard. Some teachers preprint labels with children's names and/or the date. After they write on a label, they remove it and put it in the child's Teacher File.

Legal Pads

Place small pads in several locations around the classroom so there is always one nearby. Attach a pen or pencil to the pad.

Index Cards

Index cards can be attached to a file folder with tape so that the cards overlap. Alternatively they can be color-coded by domain, stored on a ring, or filed in a box.

Calendars

Have a calendar for each month for each child on a ring. At the end of the month, file that month's calendar in each child's file. Some teachers use a weekly calendar and put notes for all students in one location. One teacher used her large desk calendar to make brief notes.

Butcher Paper

Hang butcher paper around the room above the eye levels of the students. Make notes directly on the paper or attach Post-its to it.

Masking Tape

Make notes on tape. Tear off tape and file in child's folder.

Post-it™ Notes

Post-it notes that come in a variety of sizes and colors can be attached to calendars or placed directly in students' files.

Carpenter's Aprons

Wearing a carpenter's apron enables some teachers to have Post-its and pens ready to document spontaneous as well as planned observations. Some teachers wear hats to indicate that they are observing and do not want to be disturbed unless it is an emergency.

Tape Recorders

Some teachers use a tape recorder to dictate their observations. The disadvantage of this tool is that the information must be transcribed.

PDAs and Other Computerized Devices

Teachers are beginning to use personal data assistants and other hand-held computers to input observational data. Generally these systems allow the data to be sorted by student, date, and domain.

Bibliography of Resources on Classroom Observation

Billman, J. & Sherman, J. A. (1996). *Observation and participation in early childhood settings: A practicum guide.* Needham Heights, MA: Allyn and Bacon.

Charman, C., Cross, W., & Vennis, D. (1995). *Observing children: A practical guide.* London: Cassell.

Cohen, D.H., & Stern, V. (1978). *Observing and recording the behavior of young children.* New York: Teachers College Press.

Jablon, J., Dombro, A., & Dichtelmiller, M. (1999). *The power of observation.* Washington, DC: Teaching Strategies, Inc.

Martin, S. (1994). *Take a look: Observation and portfolio assessment in early childhood.* Don Mills, Ontario: Addison-Wesley Publishers Limited.

McAfee, O. & Leong, D. (1994). *Assessing and guiding young children's development and learning.* Boston: Allyn and Bacon.

Power, B.M. (1996). *Taking note: Improving your observational notetaking.* York, ME: Stenhouse Publishers.

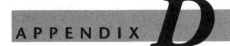

Organization of the Developmental Guidelines

Developmental Guidelines

Page 7 of the First Grade Developmental Guidelines:

Guidelines are specific to each grade level.

The domain is identified, followed by a brief description

II Language and Literacy

This domain organizes the language and literacy skills needed to understand and convey meaning into five components: Listening, Speaking, Reading, Writing, and Research. Students acquire proficiency in this domain through extensive experience with language, print, and literature in a variety of contexts. Over time students learn to construct meaning, make connections to their own lives, and gradually begin to critically analyze and interpret what they hear, observe, and read. They begin to communicate effectively orally and in writing for different audiences and purposes.

Components are labeled with letters

Performance indicators are listed numerically after component names (indicator text matches that used on the Checklist)

Each indicator is followed by a detailed rationale that describes age/grade-level expectations

Each indicator also includes several examples that illustrate some ways children might demonstrate the indicator in daily classroom activities

A Listening

1 Gains meaning by listening.

By listening, observing, and analyzing information critically, children gain understanding of the world around them. First graders are increasingly able to listen to stories read aloud, gain information, and hear directions and rules. They can listen for pleasure, information, and social interaction one-on-one, as well as in small or large groups. They can often sit for extended periods of time listening to a "good" story or presentation, but may squirm and fidget if asked to attend to something that does not immediately capture their interest. Examples of how they gain meaning by listening include:

- listening to a story read aloud and relating it to a personal experience;
- listening to a book read aloud and asking or answering a relevant question;
- listening critically as a peer retells the part of the book they heard yesterday and adding some details that she left out;

- demonstrating attentiveness and comprehension as a listener through body language or facial expressions (for example, nodding in agreement, laughing at a joke).

2 Follows multi-step directions.

Six year olds can understand and follow three- to four-step oral directions. Because they often forget or become distracted before completing a set of instructions, gentle and frequent reminders enable them to follow through to completion. Examples of how children demonstrate their increasing skill in following directions include:

- listening to someone give a series of related instructions and following them without a reminder;
- delivering a note from the teacher to the office and then waiting for an answer from the secretary before returning to the classroom;
- helping a classmate who did not hear or understand the directions by carefully repeating them;
- listening to a friend explain the directions for a game and then

playing it with few reminders about what to do next;
- hearing the choices for work time, making a decision about what to do, and then following through with the choice.

3 Demonstrates phonemic awareness.

Phonemic awareness refers to the ability to hear, think about, and manipulate the sounds in words. First graders who become successful readers can hear the smallest units of sound within words (phonemes), recognize sound segments (letter clusters, syllables), and know that words are made up of sequences of sounds. Some ways they show their ability to blend or segment phonemes include:

- hearing three distinct sounds within a word (for example, /b/ /a/ /t/ makes the word "bat");
- telling if a word sounds like another word in some way (starts the same, ends the same, or rhymes);
- saying three other words that begin with the same sound as "milk";

Core Items and Areas of Learning

Definition of Core Items

Core Items are representations (samples of work) of particular areas of learning collected within each of the following domains.

- Language and Literacy
- Mathematical Thinking
- Scientific Thinking
- Social Studies
- The Arts

These five domains lend themselves to concrete representations of student thinking. Most of our knowledge about children's status in two additional domains, Personal and Social Development and Physical Development, is learned through direct observation rather than studying children's work. These two domains, therefore, are more effectively documented on the Checklist than in the Portfolio.

The collection of Core Items in five domains ensures that the breadth of children's learning is represented and that the kinds of learning activities that have occurred in the classroom are documented. Although two areas of learning do not encompass an entire domain, if you select more than two, the Portfolio quickly becomes unmanageable because of the quantity of work being collected.

Areas of Learning

An *area of learning* is a strand of your curriculum (a part of a curriculum domain) that guides the collection of Core Items. Each domain encompasses many areas of learning. Careful selection of areas of learning results in Core Items that convey meaningful information about the quality of a child's thinking.

The responsibility for selecting areas of learning for Core Item collection rests with the teacher and school. First-hand knowledge of local curriculum and the student population is necessary to identify effective areas of learning. Some teachers prefer to define their own areas of learning; others choose from the examples offered here.

The teacher's selection of an area of learning reflects a particular understanding of how children learn. The Work Sampling System is based on the belief that children learn in an integrated way, combining many different skills and drawing on prior knowledge. This view presents a contrast to a mastery learning model in which children are expected to learn and demonstrate one skill at a time.

Effective areas of learning share the following five criteria. They

- are important parts of the curriculum,
- are specific enough to show student progress over time,
- are relevant for all students,
- reflect concepts or processes and are not dependent on particular content, and
- are most effectively documented in the Portfolio rather than on the Checklist.

Important Parts of the Curriculum

To be effective for Core Item collection, areas of learning should

- reflect an integrated set of skills, rather than a single or isolated skill,
- permit the application of several skills in a meaningful context,
- provide opportunities for many different responses (in the form of Core Items) from children, and
- invite child engagement on a daily or weekly basis.

For example, "writing to express ideas" is an effective area of learning for Core Item collection in the Language and Literacy domain. It includes such skills as use of detail and descriptive language, use of conventions of print, and sequencing and organizing ideas. On the other hand, "punctuation" is not an effective area of learning. Although it is an important skill for primary children to acquire, punctuation becomes meaningful only in the context of writing. For this reason, "writing to express ideas" is a much more useful area of learning.

Specific Enough to Show Progress over Time

To be effective, areas of learning should

- encompass a clearly identifiable progression of development, and
- be defined specifically enough to ensure that comparable work is collected during each collection period.

For example, if an area of learning in Mathematical Thinking is defined simply as "problem solving," the work collected may reflect number concepts in the fall, spatial relationships in the winter, and the use of multiple strategies to solve a problem in the spring. Clearly, the work will be different from one collection period to the next. If you are to use it to evaluate progress, however, the work from each collection period must reflect the same area of learning. Therefore, "problem solving" is too broad to be an effective area of learning for Mathematical Thinking Core Item collection. A more effective area of learning that would be specific enough to show progress over time is "using strategies to solve problems involving number concepts."

Relevant for All Students

To be effective, areas of learning should

- apply to all students regardless of their place on the developmental continuum, and
- define a wide range of performance, thus accommodating learning goals for all students in the classroom.

For example, consider the preschool teacher who initially defines "the child's application of patterning in problem solving" as an area of learning in Mathematical Thinking. As defined, this area of learning will not include those children who are just beginning to recognize attributes and to match and sort. In contrast, if the teacher defines the area of learning as "classifying, comparing, and ordering objects by attributes in order to organize them," children who are matching and sorting will be accommodated, as well as those who are recognizing and creating patterns.

Reflect Concepts or Processes

To be effective, areas of learning

- address concepts or processes that underlie or are fundamental to particular content, and
- do not reflect specific content, because curriculum changes over the course of the school year.

For example, an area of learning defined as "understanding how magnets work" is content specific. In contrast, an area of learning defined as "observing and predicting to gather scientific information" is meaningful throughout the school year because it reflects the intellectual processes that underlie studies of content such as magnetism. If an area of learning relies on specific content, once children have learned that content, the area of learning may no longer be relevant.

Best Documented in the Portfolio

To be effective, areas of learning

- require documentation of process (how children approach tasks or problems and the ways in which they represent their work) that is best shown through the Portfolio, and
- are inadequately reflected by the type of documentation that can be recorded on the Checklist (which focuses on whether a child can perform a specific skill or has acquired particular knowledge).

For example, "a child's ability to communicate through writing" requires documentation in a portfolio because it is the actual work that provides evidence of how the child is using writing to communicate. In contrast, if the area of learning had been identified as "uses letter like shapes to depict words and ideas," the teacher is responding to specific skills that can be documented quite easily in the Checklist.

Domain

II Language & Literacy	☐
III Mathematics	☐
IV Scientific Thinking	☐
V Social Studies	☐
VI The Arts	☐

Areas of Learning

Core Item Planning Worksheet

Skills and Concepts Encompassed by the Area of Learning

Classroom Activities

Child's Work/Core Items

Permission is hereby granted to reproduce pages in this Appendix for educational use.

The Work Sampling System®
©1994, 1997, 2001 Rebus Inc.

Domain	Areas of Learning	**Core Item Planning Worksheet**
II Language & Literacy ☐ III Mathematics ☒ IV Scientific Thinking ☐ V Social Studies ☐ VI The Arts ☐	Understanding of increasingly complex patterns	

Skills and Concepts Encompassed by the Area of Learning

• recognizing different types of patterns (pictures, words, movement, rhythm, number, shape)

• recognizing different patterns (AB, AAB, ABC)

• recognizing 2- and 3-D patterns

• creating original patterns

• making patterns in more than one direction (forward, backward, in a circle)

• extending and translating patterns by identifying the rule that generated the pattern

• representing and describing patterns

• using calculators to explore patterns

• making generalizations based on observed patterns

Classroom Activities	Child's Work/Core Items
Creating block patterns	Drawings, photographs, and written or dictated descriptions
Working with Unifix cubes, beads, pegboards, or other manipulative materials	Tracings, cut-out pictures, drawings, photographs, each with descriptions (written or dictated)
	Photograph with description
Block building	Drawings, paintings, written or dictated descriptions
Drawing and painting	
	Weaving with written or dictated descriptions
Weaving	Video or audio tapes, or anecdotal descriptions
Performing rhythm activities or clapping games	
Extending number patterns	Number chart, written solution to a problem

Permission is hereby granted to reproduce pages in this Appendix for educational use.

Domain	Areas of Learning	**Core Item Planning Worksheet**
II Language & Literacy ☐ III Mathematics ☐ IV Scientific Thinking ☒ V Social Studies ☐ VI The Arts ☐	Observing and recording scientific phenomena	

Skills and Concepts Encompassed by the Area of Learning

- uses more than one sense to observe
- uses scientific tools to enhance observation (magnifying lens, binoculars, microscope, weighing and measuring tools)
- makes scientific drawings with attention to detail
- tries to be realistic in scientific drawings
- uses oral and/or written descriptive language

Classroom Activities

Observing the life cycle of butterflies

Observing and recording items in a collection (e.g., shells, rocks, seeds, feathers)

Observing animal behaviors

Construction of bridges with blocks, straws, or other materials after observing them first hand

Experimentation with properties of magnets

Observing behaviors of earthworms

Child's Work/Core Items

Drawings with or without captions

Drawings, paintings, dictations, or photographs of plasticene models

Video of dramatization, drawings or paintings with dictations

Photographs of structures with descriptions

Drawn or written descriptions of observations

Anecdotal record of the child's observation, play dough models, dictated descriptions

Permission is hereby granted to reproduce pages in this Appendix for educational use.

The Work Sampling System®
©1994, 1997, 2001 Rebus Inc.

Child _____

Teacher _____ Age/Grade _____

School _____

Core Item Collection Plan

Directions: List the areas of learning in the spaces below. Make a copy of this form to include in each child's portfolio. As you add each Core Item to the portfolio, check off the appropriate collection period.

Domains	Areas of Learning	Collection Period
II **Language &** **Literacy**	1	Fall _____ Winter _____ Spring _____
	2	Fall _____ Winter _____ Spring _____
III **Mathematical** **Thinking**	1	Fall _____ Winter _____ Spring _____
	2	Fall _____ Winter _____ Spring _____
IV **Scientific** **Thinking**	1	Fall _____ Winter _____ Spring _____
	2	Fall _____ Winter _____ Spring _____
V **Social Studies**	1	Fall _____ Winter _____ Spring _____
	2	Fall _____ Winter _____ Spring _____
VI **The Arts**	1	Fall _____ Winter _____ Spring _____
	2	Fall _____ Winter _____ Spring _____

Permission is hereby granted to reproduce pages in this Appendix for educational use.

Suggestions for Core Items—Preschool and Kindergarten

To help you get started with Portfolio collection, we have provided a list of effective areas of learning for preschool and kindergarten and included examples of children's work that represent each area of learning. In some cases the examples (Core Items) are general and in others they are quite specific. We hope these ideas support your work.

Language and Literacy

AREA OF LEARNING	CHILD'S WORK/REPRESENTATION
Using symbols (e.g., symbols, drawing, emergent writing) to communicate ideas	• Scribbles created to express an idea • Child's writing (name or words) on art work • Photo of letters or symbols written in finger paint or in wet sand • Samples of copied words or written words with representational drawing or invented spelling
Communicating (verbally, manually, with gestures) to express ideas and thoughts	• Anecdotal record of story or thoughts child has expressed during group time, told to the teacher, or overheard as child talked to a friend • Record of instructions child gave to help start a game, settle an argument, or help a friend understand something • Audiotape of child telling about a school or family event
Writing (and/or dictating) to communicate ideas	• Signs made for block structures • Shopping lists made during dramatic play • Letters to friends or family members • Invitation to come to a class event • A dictated story that accompanies a drawing • Dictation of a child's description of scribbles or symbols • Copies of pages from a journal
Understanding and responding to a story	• Anecdotal record of a child retelling a story to a friend • Anecdotal notes about child acting out a story in dramatic play or on the playground • Child's depiction of a story through drawing or painting • Photo with anecdote of child "reading" a story using pictures as prompts • Record of child's responses to questions about a story • Audiotape of child retelling a story
Shows interest and understanding about books and reading	• Photo of child in reading corner for "choice time" • Photo of child at listening center • Anecdotal record of child's responses to books, questions about books or requests for books to be read • Record of child's use of books to obtain information about how to build a bridge or a castle • Record of child's conversation with others about books or stories • Child's dictated thoughts about a story

The Work Sampling System®
©1994, 1997, 2001 Rebus Inc.

Permission is hereby granted to reproduce pages in this Appendix for educational use.

Mathematical Thinking

AREA OF LEARNING	CHILD'S WORK/REPRESENTATION
Understanding and applying classification and seriation skills	• Record of child sorting beads • Photo of child's arrangement of rods, buttons, or crayons in order of size • Photo of child putting away blocks or other equipment according to size, shape, or use • Anecdotal record of child's comment about the rule used for classifying • Anecdotal record of child's comments at snack or out on the playground that demonstrate understanding of seriation or classification • Child's drawing that shows classifying skills (these are all toys, this is my family, or these are all the kinds of leaves we collected) • A collage of categorized items (e.g., shapes, colors, foods, animals, or "the things we do on the playground")
Understanding and using number concepts to solve problems	• Anecdote describing child's method of arranging cups and napkins for snack • Description of child counting children at sand table to see if there is room for a friend • Record of child's solution to a question about distributing class supplies for a project • Record of child's counting children at circle and remarking that "there are more girls than boys"
Understanding and applying size and measurements concepts	• Record of child's comments comparing sizes of blocks • Photo with note of child measuring own height or the growth of a plant • Anecdote depicting how child compared heights of classmates • Photo of child measuring amounts of ingredients during a cooking project, potting plants, or making play dough • Child-created measuring tape for determining the length of a block structure or the snack table • Photo of child using balance scale

Permission is hereby granted to reproduce pages in this Appendix for educational use.

The Work Sampling System®
©1994, 1997, 2001 Rebus Inc.

Using sorting, classifying, and patterning skills	• Photo of pattern created with pattern blocks or other manipulatives: sample of patterning using collage materials
	• Anecdotal record of comments about a pattern or classification grouping within the class ("all the people with red socks should sit over there and people with other colored socks sit here")
	• Record of clapping pattern or motor pattern
	• Photo of beads, rods, or buttons arranged in a pattern or sorted according to a specific attribute
	• Photo of pattern created with finger paint or in shaving cream
	• Photo of peg board patterns
	• Paper replicas of created patterns

Permission is hereby granted to reproduce pages in this Appendix for educational use.

Scientific Thinking

AREA OF LEARNING	CHILD'S WORK/REPRESENTATION
Using senses to explore and observe the natural and physical world	• Anecdotal record or child's comments when playing with water or sand toys, pounding play dough, exploring glue, finger paints, or shaving cream • Record of child's responses to group recall of sounds heard on the woods walk or sites seen on the library walk • Child's dictated observation of the class pet, seeds sprouting, or objects on the magnet board • Photo of child's exploration of a bird's nest
Observing and predicting (or guessing) in an investigation	• A record of seed growth including child-made chart and comments about what helps the plant to grow • Dictated guess about what will float and what will sink and why • Record of child's prediction about weight of objects • Record of child's guesses or predictions during a class brainstorming discussion • Interview with the child about predictions of what the bunny will eat and how to find out if the prediction is accurate
Experimenting and solving problems during exploration	• Child-created chart that describes what the class pet eats and drinks for a week and determination for what to feed it next week • Chart or record of plant growth including experimentation with amounts of sun, water, plant food • Photo with accompanying note showing the child's experimentation at the water table with different sized tubes to determine the one that makes the water flow fastest, the child's prediction, and the child's description of the result
Observing and describing the environment	• Drawing of child's collection of leaves • Drawn and dictated observations of the behaviors of the class pet • Photo and anecdote of child's observations of what is heard when listening through a stethoscope or looking through a magnifying glass • Child's description of how play dough feels, or how a new kind of cracker or fruit tastes • Photo and record of child's observation when blowing bubbles

Permission is hereby granted to reproduce pages in this Appendix for educational use.

The Work Sampling System®
©1994, 1997, 2001 Rebus Inc.

Social Studies

AREA OF LEARNING	CHILD'S WORK/REPRESENTATION
Gathering and interpreting information about families and the community	• Painting or collage of family members • Drawing of trip to a hospital or police station • Drawing and writing about a family vacation • Photo depicting child's role play of a family member in the housekeeping area • Photo of child's block structure of the airport, their house, or church
Collecting and interpreting information about people's roles in a community	• Record of child's "interview" with the school custodian or principal, doctor, or a shoe salesperson • Child's response during a brainstorming session about the jobs of community workers • Anecdote describing the child's reenactment of a visit to the grocer or the pharmacist • Photo of child's train made from chairs or big blocks, diagram of a shoe store created with unit blocks
Developing knowledge and understanding about self and family	• Drawing or painting of child's depiction of family working or playing • Dictated story about a family party, argument, or trip • Child's book or collage of family members and their activities • Photo and note showing the child's reenactment of family interactions • Anecdote of child's description of how the work gets done at his house
Recognizing and understanding similarities and differences among people	• Drawing of friends who are different from each other • Child's comment, as recorded and initialed on the experience chart, about the ways people are different from or similar to each other • Anecdote documenting a snack table discussion about similarities and differences in families' activities

Permission is hereby granted to reproduce pages in this Appendix for educational use.

The Arts

AREA OF LEARNING	CHILD'S WORK/REPRESENTATION
Participating in visual arts (or dramatic arts, or music, or dance/creative movement)	• Drawings (e.g., with pencils, chalk, markers, or crayons) • Paintings (e.g., with tempera, watercolors, or finger paint) • Photo of clay or play dough sculptures • Photo of child dancing or singing • Anecdote or audiotape of child-created song • Photo of child dramatizing with puppet or felt board • Collage with dictation of child's explanation of how it was created
Using the arts to represent ideas	• Drawings • Paintings • Photo of child telling a story through dance or movement • Anecdote or audiotape of child's musical retelling of a story • Audiotape of child singing about a class or family event
Exploring different artistic media	• Samples of child's work with a variety of art media • Collage with anecdotal notes of child's verbal explanation about the collage • Sample of child's cut-out magazine pictures or use of scissors to create a design • Photo of child's creative dancing or puppet show story
Exploring and using a single art medium	• Examples of child's work in easel painting or marker drawings throughout the year • Photos and anecdotal record of child's progress in communicating through dance or dramatization • Photos of child's representations made with clay or play dough • Collage work collected over the year • Audiotapes of child singing over the course of the year • Audiotapes of child using a classroom instrument over the year such as rhythm sticks, a triangle, or a kazoo

Permission is hereby granted to reproduce pages in this Appendix for educational use.

The Work Sampling System®
©1994, 1997, 2001 Rebus Inc.

Suggestions for Core Items—Elementary-Grades

To help you get started with Portfolio collection, we have provided a list of effective areas of learning for elementary grades and included examples of children's work that represent each area of learning. In some cases the examples (Core Items) are general and in others they are quite specific. We hope these ideas support your work.

Language and Literacy

AREA OF LEARNING	CHILD'S WORK/REPRESENTATION
Communicating ideas verbally	• An audiotape of the student doing an oral research presentation describing a scientific investigation • Dictation of the student's spoken language • Artwork with dictation of the child's description of the work • Dictation of the student's contributions to a class discussion • An anecdote that captures a direct quotation of student's language • An audiotape or dictation of an interview with the student
Using strategies to read for meaning-decoding and expressing	• An audiotape of the student reading aloud accompanied by the teacher's description of strategies being used • A running record or miscue analysis of text read by the student with a guide to help parents understand it • An interview with the student about his reading strategies
Comprehending and interpreting text	• A book report • An illustration of a story with writing or dictation • A story map of a book • Written or verbal responses to questions about a story or other text • A written or dictated letter to the author about one of the author's books • A written or dictated review of a book • A re-write or re-telling of a story or the ending to a story
Writing to express ideas	• A story, poem, or fable written by the student • A journal entry • A script for a skit or puppet show • An article for the class newspaper • A letter • A research report • A sign for a block structure or model

Permission is hereby granted to reproduce pages in this Appendix for educational use.

The Work Sampling System®
©1994, 1997, 2001 Rebus Inc.

Mathematical Thinking

AREA OF LEARNING	CHILD'S WORK/REPRESENTATION
Using strategies to solve number problems	• The student's drawing, chart, graph, calculations, and solution to a word problem, with an explanation of the process in the student's words • An anecdotal record of a student's approach to solving a number problem • A videotape or an audiotape, showing the student's approach to solving a number problem • A student-created word problem(s) that illustrates a number sentence or equation
Using strategies to solve problems involving geometrical concepts	• A student's pictorial representation (or photo) and verbal description of the solution to a problem using Tangrams, Pattern Blocks, Pentominoes or other geometry materials • An anecdote of the student's process and solution to a geometry problem • A student's written description of her process and solution to a geometry problem • A photo or student-drawn representation of a solution to a geoboard problem • A photo or sketch of two and three-dimensional shapes made from pipe cleaners or straws • Student's analysis of the use of shapes in the environment or in the construction of a building
Solving problems involving number concepts and arithmetic operations	• Photos or student-drawn representations of numbers or operations, using manipulatives • Samples of written computations • A teacher-written anecdote or the student's written description about the student's use of number concepts and operations • A photo or anecdote of the student using Cuisenaire Rods to represent numbers and to perform numerical operations • Collage of magazine pictures showing different quantities of objects, with number sentences written to accompany them • Photo or pictorial representation of the value of sets of coins

Applying the concept of patterns and relationships to problem-solving	• Photo or student-made replica of a copied, original, or extended pattern • An anecdote of a student's recognition of a geometrical, numerical, or natural pattern • Dictated or student-written analysis of the patterns and relationships in a numerical sequence, a two or three-dimensional design, or a naturally occurring arrangement • Artwork that incorporates sorting, patterning, sequencing, balance, and symmetry
Applying measurement concepts to solve real world problems	• Photograph, with dictated or student-written explanation, of a student using unifix cubes to compare heights of classmates • An anecdote describing a student's method of doubling the measurements in a recipe • Student's calculations made while figuring how many pounds of hamburger to get for the class picnic • Diagram or drawing that shows how much wood is needed to complete a woodworking project
Applying estimation strategies in measurement, computation, and problem-solving	• Student's description of the strategies used to estimate the number of objects in a container • A photograph with anecdotal note describing a student pacing off an estimated 100 yards for a running race • A student's estimated range of numbers that could be the answer to a word problem, along with the actual solution • A written or dictated estimate, with the reason for that estimate, of how long it will be before all the snow melts from the playground or how long it will take for the plant to produce a flower

Permission is hereby granted to reproduce pages in this Appendix for educational use.

The Work Sampling System®
©1994, 1997, 2001 Rebus Inc.

Scientific Thinking

AREA OF LEARNING	CHILD'S WORK/REPRESENTATION
Observing, recording, and describing phenomena	• A drawing or painting, with written or dictated description of a classroom pet, a natural object, or plant • A written or dictated description of an observed event or process • A sketch of an object, as seen under a magnifying lens or microscope, with labels to identify parts • Comparative drawings that show differences among trees, animals, people, rocks, shells, or feathers
Collecting and communicating scientific data about change over time	• Excerpts from a science log, tracking the growth of a plant over time • A series of drawings showing the metamorphosis of a caterpillar or tadpole • A series of descriptions of mold over several days • A collection of data describing cloud color, size, formation, and accompanying weather conditions over time
Interpreting and explaining information generated by scientific investigation	• Written or dictated explanations after observing animal or plant behavior in different situations • Pictures and explanations of changes in a cake before and after baking or an oil/water mixture before and after stirring • Photos of model bridges made in different ways, the results of weight-bearing tests, and written or dictated interpretation of the findings • Audio or videotaped presentation of findings from an investigation about the absorbency, buoyancy, and fluidity of different liquids
Investigating a question by predicting, testing, explaining, and drawing conclusions	• Written or dictated prediction to a question about the causes of natural disasters, along with written, drawn, or dictated information from research that supports or negates the prediction • An anecdotal record of a student's questions and efforts to find answers • A student's description of an experiment designed to answer a classmate's question about food preferences of different wild birds • An excerpt from a science log, showing three possible ways to collect information to answer a question about electricity
Planning and conducting an experiment to answer a question or to test a hypothesis	• Photo and anecdotal note of student conducting informal experiments at the water table • Student-written or dictated descriptions of two ramps built in the block area in order to test which toy car rolled the farthest • Student's written description and steps of an experiment designed to compare the weights of different substances • A written summary of a scientific experiment with insects, including the student's hypothesis and newly discovered information

The Work Sampling System®
©1994, 1997, 2001 Rebus Inc.

Permission is hereby granted to reproduce pages in this Appendix for educational use.

Social Studies

AREA OF LEARNING	CHILD'S WORK/REPRESENTATION
Collecting and understanding information about self and family	• Student-written or dictated description of her/himself and her/his family • Drawing that reveals knowledge of family terminology and functions • A life book or timeline that tracks the student's life or the life of a family member • A photograph of the student with a written, taped, or dictated autobiography
Understanding human interdependence in communities (e.g., family, classroom, school community, nation)	• Written or dictated story depicting characters who depend on one another • Drawings and descriptions of various jobs and their importance in the community • A written or taped analysis of a book or story about people who work together to achieve a goal • Anecdotal record of student participation in a classroom economy • Text and interpretation of an interview with a community leader
Collecting, understanding, and interpreting information about the relationship between people and their environment	• Anecdotal evidence of a student's knowledge about pollution: verbal contributions to discussions, description of recycling efforts made by the student, newspaper articles the student brought in • Photograph with accompanying description of a model of the local community showing how and where people live and work • Drawings of people's home who live in different climates • Interviews with people about the effects of local factories on their lives and a summary of the information gathered through the interviews • A research report about eco-systems
Using maps and other geographic representations	• Anecdotal note of a student's use of a map, atlas, or globe to locate a city, state, country, or body of water • A student's hand-drawn map, made to give directions to her house or to find objects in a scavenger hunt • A photograph of a three-dimensional model of the school yard, the neighborhood, or community that shows actual geographic features • A record of comparisons between old and modern maps of the same area

Permission is hereby granted to reproduce pages in this Appendix for educational use.

The Work Sampling System
©1994, 1997, 2001 Rebus Inc.

Collecting, understanding, and interpreting information related to social studies topics	• Information and summary from interview with a senior citizen about long ago life • Research report about an historical figure or event, a political controversy, or a different culture or country • Drawing or text, summarizing a video about different kinds of families, an incident of discrimination, or a human conflict • Dialogue of conversation about different celebrations, different eating habits, different viewpoints about a group of people • An historical fiction story about an era or conflict in the past
Understanding and interpreting information about the relationship between people and their surroundings	• Research report about how a historical group of people used resources from the environment to shape their culture • Drawings or paintings depicting how people live and work (e.g., the homes of people who live in the desert, transportation methods used by people who live in the Arctic region, how the river is used for employment) • A story written by the student describing life in early America

Permission is hereby granted to reproduce pages in this Appendix for educational use.

The Arts

AREA OF LEARNING	CHILD'S WORK/REPRESENTATION
Using the arts to represent ideas	• A painting that tells a story • A drawing with written or dictated text • A tape of a song made up by a student to describe a field trip • A videotape of a student-created skit
Responding to, interpreting, and analyzing artistic experiences	• Writing about personal reactions to the art seen on a museum field trip • A drawing that expresses how an artistic work or performance made the student feel • A record of comments from a discussion of a play the class saw • Videotape of children recreating the choreography of a dance they saw performed by a professional dance troupe • A student's written notes from an interview of another student about an artistic event they both attended
Understanding the arts as an expression of history and culture	• A reproduction of a mask, weaving, or style of painting from a different culture • Written or dictated explanation about why an art form was practiced by an ancient culture • A photo of a banner or flag designed by the student to represent the unique qualities of his family, school, or town
Exploring and controlling an artistic medium	• Paintings collected at various times throughout the year • Sculptures made from different materials collected over the course of the year • Collages collected over the course of the year • Crayon drawings made over time • Audiotape of a student playing a musical instrument at different times during the year

Permission is hereby granted to reproduce pages in this Appendix for educational use.

The Work Sampling System®
©1994, 1997, 2001 Rebus Inc.

Examples of Completed Summary Reports

CHILD _____   AGE/GRADE _____

TEACHER _____   DATE _____

SCHOOL _____

ATTENDANCE: DAYS TARDY _____   DAYS ABSENT _____

The Work Sampling System®
Summary Report

FALL ☐
WINTER ☐
YEAR-END ☐

WHITE – FAMILY   YELLOW – OFFICE   PINK – TEACHER

GENERAL COMMENTS: Give reasons for "Needs Development" and/or note special strengths and talents in each domain. Also give explanation if progress is other than expected. Describe plans for supporting child's growth.

PROGRESS

Expected
Other than Expected
As Expected

PERFORMANCE

PORTFOLIO
Needs Development
As Expected

CHECKLIST
Needs Development
As Expected

DOMAINS & COMPONENTS

I Personal & Social Development
Self concept
Self control
Approaches to learning
Interaction with others
Social problem-solving

II Language & Literacy
Listening
Speaking
Reading
Writing
Research (3–5)

III Mathematical Thinking
Mathematical processes
Number and operations
Patterns, relationships, and functions
Geometry and spatial relations
Measurement
Data collection and probability (K–5)

IV Scientific Thinking
Inquiry
Physical science (K–5)
Life science (K–5)
Earth science (K–5)

V Social Studies
People, past and present
Human interdependence
Citizenship and government
People and where they live

VI The Arts
Expression and representation
Understanding and appreciation

VII Physical Development & Health
Gross motor development
Fine motor development
Personal health and safety

4th Edition   ©1997, 2001 Rebus Inc.

SEE REVERSE FOR HOW TO READ THE SUMMARY REPORT

The Work Sampling System®
©2001 Rebus Inc.

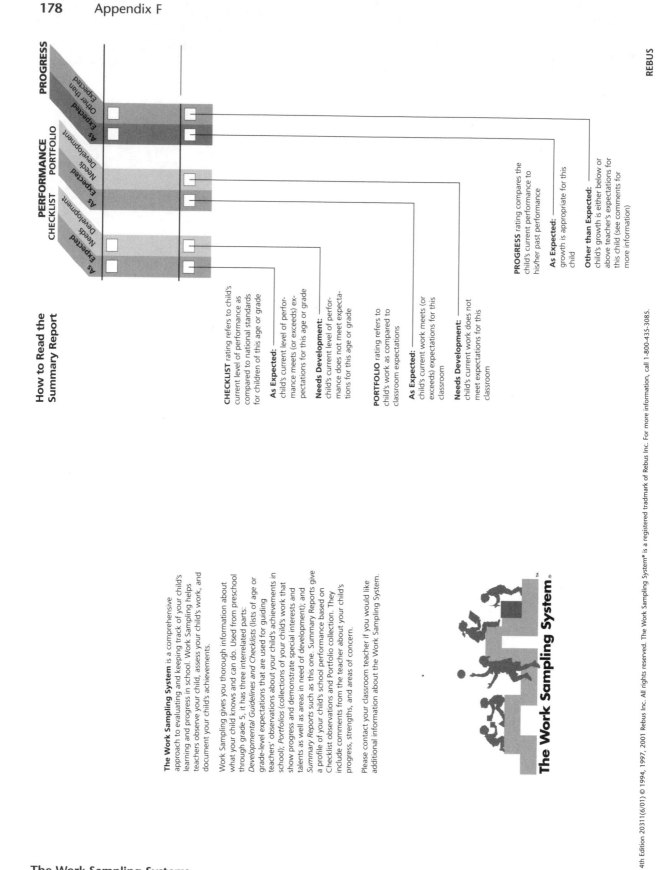

How to Read the Summary Report

The Work Sampling System is a comprehensive approach to evaluating and keeping track of your child's learning and progress in school. Work Sampling helps teachers observe your child, assess your child's work, and document your child's achievements.

Work Sampling gives you thorough information about what your child knows and can do. Used from preschool through grade 5, it has three interrelated parts: *Developmental Guidelines and Checklists* (lists of age or grade-level expectations that are used for guiding teachers' observations about your child's achievements in school); *Portfolios* (collections of your child's work that show progress and demonstrate special interests and talents as well as areas in need of development); and *Summary Reports* such as this one. Summary Reports give a profile of your child's school performance based on Checklist observations and Portfolio collection. They include comments from the teacher about your child's progress, strengths, and areas of concern.

Please contact your classroom teacher if you would like additional information about the Work Sampling System.

CHECKLIST rating refers to child's current level of performance as compared to national standards for children of this age or grade

As Expected:
child's current level of performance meets (or exceeds) expectations for this age or grade

Needs Development:
child's current level of performance does not meet expectations for this age or grade

PORTFOLIO rating refers to child's work as compared to classroom expectations

As Expected:
child's current work meets (or exceeds) expectations for this classroom

Needs Development:
child's current work does not meet expectations for this classroom

PROGRESS rating compares the child's current performance to his/her past performance

As Expected:
growth is appropriate for this child

Other than Expected:
child's growth is either below or above teacher's expectations for this child (see comments for more information)

The Work Sampling System®

The Work Sampling System®

©2001 Rebus Inc.

4th Edition 20311(6/01) © 1994, 1997, 2001 Rebus Inc. All rights reserved. The Work Sampling System® is a registered tradmark of Rebus Inc. For more information, call 1-800-435-3085.

REBUS

CHILD _Kenneth Hampton_   AGE/GRADE _Pre-Primary_

TEACHER _Rider_   DATE _3/5/95_

SCHOOL _Westview Early Childhood Center_

ATTENDANCE: DAYS TARDY _____   DAYS ABSENT _____

The Work Sampling System.
Summary Report

FALL ☐
WINTER ☑
YEAR-END ☐

PROGRESS

GENERAL COMMENTS: Give reasons for "Needs Development" and/or note special strengths and talents in each domain. Also give explanation if progress is other than expected. Describe plans for supporting child's growth.

I Personal & Social Development
Self concept
Self control
Approaches to learning
Interaction with others
Social problem-solving

Kenny is excited about learning activities in the classroom. At times he can interact well with other children and adults. Kenny has made little progress in learning how to resolve conflicts, follow directions, and use words to express anger and continues to need my support in these areas. One way I am helping him is through small group activities that focus on feelings.

II Language & Literacy
Listening
Speaking
Reading
Writing
Research (3-5)

Kenny loves books, listening to stories, and is just starting to work on writing. He uses his name card to practice writing letters. When speaking, he struggles to put words together and to verbally communicate with others. As we have discussed, he is receiving some outside support to help him develop these skills.

III Mathematical Thinking
Mathematical processes
Number and operations
Patterns, relationships, and functions
Geometry and spatial relations
Measurement
Data collection and probability (K-5)

Kenny is very interested in quantities and numbers. He can easily recognize and copy simple patterns. Kenny can also accurately count with 1-to-1 correspondence up to 5.

IV Scientific Thinking
Inquiry
Physical science (K-5)
Life science (K-5)
Earth science (K-5)

Kenny enjoys using his senses to explore the world around him. He is very observant, draws pictures of what he sees, and tries to use his words to describe or question what he discovers. Kenny is also beginning to understand and interpret information on a chart.

V Social Studies
People, past and present
Human interdependence
Citizenship and government
People and where they live

Kenny is beginning to understand family roles. He talks of his family often. There was concern for a few months (Nov.-Jan.) as Kenny did not adjust well to the new baby at home. He has shown considerable progress and is beginning to talk about how he takes care of the baby.

VI The Arts
Expression and representation
Understanding and appreciation

Kenny loves music and finger plays. He is very responsive to them and this could greatly aid his language development. Kenny also enjoys acting out stories.

VII Physical Development & Health
Gross motor development
Fine motor development
Personal health and safety

Kenny is right on target for a four-year-old. He can jump, run, hop and climb with great balance and coordination. He is working on his fine motor skills by working with puzzles, blocks and manipulatives.

DOMAINS & COMPONENTS

PERFORMANCE
CHECKLIST / PORTFOLIO

As Expected / Needs Development

SEE REVERSE FOR HOW TO READ THE SUMMARY REPORT

4th Edition   ©1997, 2001 Rebus Inc.

WHITE – FAMILY   YELLOW – OFFICE   PINK – TEACHER

The Work Sampling System®
©2001 Rebus Inc.

CHILD _Christina Paxton_   **AGE/GRADE** _Age. 4.8_

TEACHER _Terry Jackson_   **DATE** _June 1994_

SCHOOL _____

ATTENDANCE: DAYS TARDY _____ **DAYS ABSENT** _8_

The Work Sampling System®
Summary Report

FALL ☐
WINTER ☑
YEAR-END ☐

PROGRESS

GENERAL COMMENTS: Give reasons for "Needs Development" and/or note special strengths and talents in each domain. Also give explanation if progress is other than expected. Describe plans for supporting child's growth.

I Personal & Social Development
Self concept
Self control
Approaches to learning
Interaction with others
Social problem-solving

Christina's sense of self grows. She exchanges ideas freely with other children. Her comfort grows at entering a new play area and finding a role for herself that fits the play of others. She follows the classroom rules that she remembers. Transitions are manageable except following vacations. Christina is a curious and eager learner. She interacts cooperatively in a group although she prefers 1-1 relationships. She is very empathetic toward others. Songs, finger plays, and group games generally have appeal.

II Language & Literacy
Listening
Speaking
Reading
Writing
Research (3-5)

Christina works at listening with understanding when adults are talking to a group. She speaks clearly and uses language for a variety of purposes. Stories engage Christina and she especially prefers 1-1 reading activities. She is quite interested in writing activities, forming many letters, making lists, and drawing shapes. She writes her own name.

III Mathematical Thinking
Mathematical processes
Number and operations
Patterns, relationships, and functions
Geometry and spatial relations
Measurement
Data collection and probability (K-5)

Christina engages in discussions around quantity and number: "I'm 4-1/2," she says. She is able to duplicate simple patterns with blocks and sorts colors and shapes. She works at seriation: small, medium, and large. She makes 1-1 correspondence with 1-5 objects. Christina identifies many shapes: ○, △ She understands positional and comparative words and enjoys measuring activities. She's beginning to develop a sense of time.

IV Scientific Thinking
Inquiry
Physical science (K-5)
Life science (K-5)
Earth science (K-5)

Christina enjoys using her senses to observe the world around her. Her questions and predictions indicate her ability to compare. She seeks answers through active exploration.

V Social Studies
People, past and present
Human interdependence
Citizenship and government
People and where they live

Christina recognizes her own physical characteristics and those of others. She begins to understand family structures different from her own. She speaks with understanding about some community helpers, e.g., firemen, telephone men. She has a sense for the reasons for rules in the community and what happens when people don't pick up their own mess. She enjoys locating common household items in their place in the doll house.

VI The Arts
Expression and representation
Understanding and appreciation

Christina uses a variety of materials for exploration. She participates in group music experiences more often than she did at the beginning of the year. She enjoys watching the work of others. She often chooses to be an observer rather than a participant.

VII Physical Development & Health
Gross motor development
Fine motor development
Personal health and safety

Christina works at refining her balance and control. She is able to hop on one foot. She works at catching a ball with two hands and climbing with assurance. Self-help skills improve slowly. Christina works at the water table twisting and pouring. Eye-hand coordination appears well developed for her age. She enjoys puzzles and construction with manipulatives. She exhibits control with markers and brushes and works at combining these skills in an organized way.

DOMAINS & COMPONENTS

PERFORMANCE — CHECKLIST — PORTFOLIO
Needs Development / As Expected / Other than Expected

SEE REVERSE FOR HOW TO READ THE SUMMARY REPORT

4th Edition   ©1997, 2001 Rebus Inc

WHITE – FAMILY   YELLOW – OFFICE   PINK – TEACHER

The Work Sampling System®
©2001 Rebus Inc.

CHILD Allison Fromm **AGE/GRADE** Kindergarten

TEACHER Donna House **DATE** February 1994

SCHOOL _____

ATTENDANCE: DAYS TARDY _____ **DAYS ABSENT** 2

The Work Sampling System.
Summary Report

FALL ☐
WINTER ☑
YEAR-END ☐

GENERAL COMMENTS: Give reasons for "Needs Development" and/or note special strengths and talents in each domain. Also give explanation if progress is other than expected. Describe plans for supporting child's growth.

PERFORMANCE — CHECKLIST / PORTFOLIO
(As Expected / Needs Development)

PROGRESS — As Expected / Other than Expected

DOMAINS & COMPONENTS

I Personal & Social Development
Self concept
Self control
Approaches to learning
Interaction with others
Social problem-solving

Allison's self-confidence has grown significantly since the fall. She talks more often, usually with one other, shares playthings and even silliness with children and adults, and chooses a variety of activities during Choice Time. Overall, she appears animated and happy. If a conflict arises, she usually expresses her feelings to a teacher. This is a great step compared to her lack of sharing feelings in the fall. A goal will be to help her resolve conflicts directly with her peers first, then seek adult help if needed.

II Language & Literacy
Listening
Speaking
Reading
Writing
Research (3-5)

Books still hold her interest yet her comprehension is minimal. Her recall of details is better but predicting/interpreting information is lacking. Allison's drawings have increased slightly in detail and she's beginning to copy words for her stories. Just recently, she has begun to ask questions of her peers during group settings. This is exciting! Allison's attention span during group discussion is short. She frequently escapes to the bathroom. Allison continues to receive speech/language and reading services during the week. Clearly, her vocabulary and expression have grown rapidly.

III Mathematical Thinking
Mathematical processes
Number and operations
Patterns, relationships, and functions
Geometry and spatial relations
Measurement
Data collection and probability (K-5)

Allison can sort objects by color and shape with some guidance from an adult. She can label objects "big" and "small"; however, it is difficult for her to order objects by size. She can count to five when pointing to each object in a group. Allison has made only slight progress in her math readiness skills. She will continue to work on these individually and with the class.

IV Scientific Thinking
Inquiry
Physical science (K-5)
Life science (K-5)
Earth science (K-5)

Allison was actively involved in our research of forest animals. She enjoyed looking at her "bear" books especially. She drew many pictures of bears and forests. Several of her easel paintings included browns and greens and she told me that they were forest paintings.

V Social Studies
People, past and present
Human interdependence
Citizenship and government
People and where they live

Allison seemed to enjoy sharing her museum with her peers. She was eager to bring in family objects from home and had many details to tell about them. Her understanding of family/community roles is growing.

VI The Arts
Expression and representation
Understanding and appreciation

Allison enjoys using art materials in the classroom. Allison's participation in our storytelling residency was active for about 10 minutes (each session), then unfocused. Her singing participation is increasing.

VII Physical Development & Health
Gross motor development
Fine motor development
Personal health and safety

Gross and fine motor skills are developing gradually. She is beginning to use the climbing equipment on the playground as long as an adult is close by. She is beginning to use the scissors and staplers successfully. She holds a pencil correctly and can form letters.

WHITE – FAMILY   YELLOW – OFFICE   PINK – TEACHER

4th Edition ©1997, 2001 Rebus Inc.

SEE REVERSE FOR HOW TO READ THE SUMMARY REPORT

The Work Sampling System®
©2001 Rebus Inc.

CHILD _Donald Thompson_

TEACHER _Carrie Henry_

SCHOOL _____

ATTENDANCE: DAYS TARDY _____   **DAYS ABSENT** _4_

AGE/GRADE _First Grade_

DATE _February 1994_

The Work Sampling System.
Summary Report

FALL ☐
WINER ☑
YEAR-END ☐

PROGRESS

GENERAL COMMENTS: Give reasons for "Needs Development" and/or note special strengths and talents in each domain. Also give explanation if progress is other than expected. Describe plans for supporting child's growth.

PERFORMANCE
CHECKLIST   PORTFOLIO

DOMAINS & COMPONENTS

I Personal & Social Development
Self concept
Self control
Approaches to learning
Interaction with others
Social problem-solving

Don has the potential for being an eager learner. He shows interest and curiosity in topics we study and has many good ideas to share. I am concerned about the ways in which his behavior interferes with his learning. During class meetings, at Choice Time, and during work time he challenges classroom rules and distracts others. I am continuing to work with Don about taking responsibility for his actions. Although he has not made progress in this area during the past few months, I hope we can all work together to help Don focus on his enthusiasm for learning and gain some control over his behavior.

II Language & Literacy
Listening
Speaking
Reading
Writing
Research (3-5)

When he is focused, Don can be a good listener and can contribute information to discussions. His oral language has improved. Don developed several reading strategies as a result of his involvement with the Reading Recovery Program. However he avoids reading in class and has made little progress since he finished the program. I am encouraging Don to read at home and will continue to suggest books related to sports, a topic I know he enjoys. His writing has improved since the beginning of the year, both the content and the mechanics. Although the process of writing is difficult for him, he is proud of the short sequenced stories he creates.

III Mathematical Thinking
Mathematical processes
Number and operations
Patterns, relationships, and functions
Geometry and spatial relations
Measurement
Data collection and probability (K-5)

Don's strength in mathematics is with number concepts. He creates and solves challenging problems using numbers from the calendar. Using math manipulatives, Don does double digit addition with regrouping. He has started to do some mental problem solving. During the last month we have been working on spatial thinking using Tangrams. He gets frustrated and gives up when he can't manipulate the shapes to fit into the design. I will continue to work with him on developing spatial reasoning skills.

IV Scientific Thinking
Inquiry
Physical science (K-5)
Life science (K-5)
Earth science (K-5)

Our study of animals and habitats appealed to Don. He learned a great deal of specific information and understands the concepts of camouflage and predator/prey relationships. He is able to classify animals according to categories. He observes scientific phenomena with increasing attention to detail as seen by his efforts to create detailed and accurate drawings. It is a challenge for him to write about his scientific observations.

V Social Studies
People, past and present
Human interdependence
Citizenship and government
People and where they live

We have studied various habitats and considered the ways in which environment affects how people live and work. Don demonstrates a basic understanding of the differences in types of habitats through his block building and model making with plasticene.

VI The Arts
Expression and representation
Understanding and appreciation

Don expresses ideas through the use of construction materials, such as large blocks and legos. Because he is still developing fine motor skills, drawing and painting present a challenge for him. He enjoys using stencils and stamps as an alternative to drawing with markers and pencils. He listens carefully to music and spends time observing the artwork of others.

VII Physical Development & Health
Gross motor development
Fine motor development
Personal health and safety

Don loves gross motor activities. He looks forward to gym and recess and works hard to improve skills such as ball handling, kicking, and batting. He struggles with fine motor skills which interferes with his ability to express his thinking in writing or with drawing, but he is making slow and steady progress.

SEE REVERSE FOR HOW TO READ THE SUMMARY REPORT   4th Edition   ©1997, 2001 Rebus Inc.

WHITE – FAMILY   YELLOW – OFFICE   PINK – TEACHER

The Work Sampling System®

©2001 Rebus Inc.

CHILD _Theresa Jones_   AGE/GRADE _Second Grade_

TEACHER _Paulina Richardson_   DATE _February 1994_

SCHOOL _____

ATTENDANCE: DAYS TARDY _____   DAYS ABSENT _5_

The Work Sampling System.
Summary Report

FALL ☐
WINTER ☑
YEAR-END ☐

PROGRESS

GENERAL COMMENTS: Give reasons for "Needs Development" and/or note special strengths and talents in each domain. Also give explanation if progress is other than expected. Describe plans for supporting child's growth.

Theresa has many friends who are drawn to her because she is energetic and enthusiastic. Because she tends to insist on having her own way, her relationships with peers are fraught with tension and she often challenges adult authority. Theresa shows interest in new topics presented in class but has difficulty sustaining interest in a subject over time, as seen by comments during class discussions such as, "are we still studying that?" My goals for Theresa are for her to become more persistent and willing to engage in in-depth study. I have been conferencing with her independently, trying to find ways to capture her interest in classroom topics.

Theresa has wonderful strength as a reader and speller. She reads a variety of texts and uses conventional spelling in her writing with reasonable accuracy. I would like to see her develop better listening skills. Because she is easily distracted, she misses the details of what is happening in stories and discussions. While Theresa enjoys writing, she begins many more stories than she actually completes. She doesn't like to read over her stories to check for organization and logic. I have been working with her on organizing stories so that they have a clear beginning, middle, and end.

Theresa has a firm grasp on place value and regrouping (in addition and subtraction) and can apply these concepts in problem solving. She is increasingly able to solve problems in her head, relying less on manipulative materials. She is an active participant in our daily calendar quiz, both as a problem solver- and inventor. We have been working with Tangrams on spatial thinking this term. Theresa attacks new problems with enthusiasm but tends to give up if her first attempts do not produce a workable solution.

Theresa has learned some basic concepts about animals and habitats. As an observer, she notices and records what can be easily seen. I am working with her to observe carefully and for longer periods of time so that she can note and record specific details. It is difficult for Theresa to incorporate previously learned information to new situations. I am encouraging her to read non-fiction books about animals and where they live to reinforce some of the concepts of our study.

In our study of habitats, we have investigated how various environments affect how people live and work. In her attempts (stories, paintings, and dioramas) to represent her understanding of what has been studied. Theresa continues to rely heavily on her imagination, rather than incorporating factual information and ideas studied in class. I am supporting her growth in this area by conferencing with her prior to field trips, discussions, stories, and videos to help her focus her attention on at least one main idea or event from each experience.

Theresa has many wonderful ideas about how to express herself artistically. She enjoys making puppets and painting. She loves to sing and participates enthusiastically in classroom and all school sings.

Theresa has strong gross and fine motor skills. She enjoys jump roping at recess and does it with confidence and skill. She is capable of precise neat work.

	PERFORMANCE				PROGRESS	
DOMAINS & COMPONENTS	CHECKLIST		PORTFOLIO			
	As Expected	Needs Development	As Expected	Needs Development	As Expected	Other than Expected
I Personal & Social Development						☑
Self concept						
Self control						
Approaches to learning						
Interaction with others						
Social problem-solving						
II Language & Literacy	☑		☑		☑	
Listening						
Speaking						
Reading						
Writing						
Research (3-5)						
III Mathematical Thinking	☑		☑		☑	
Mathematical processes						
Number and operations						
Patterns, relationships, and functions						
Geometry and spatial relations						
Measurement						
Data collection and probability (K-5)						
IV Scientific Thinking	☑		☑		☑	
Inquiry						
Physical science (K-5)						
Life science (K-5)						
Earth science (K-5)						
V Social Studies	☑	☑	☑			☑
People, past and present						
Human interdependence						
Citizenship and government						
People and where they live						
VI The Arts	☑		☑			☑
Expression and representation						
Understanding and appreciation						
VII Physical Development & Health	☑		☑			☑
Gross motor development						
Fine motor development						
Personal health and safety						

WHITE – FAMILY   YELLOW – OFFICE   PINK – TEACHER

SEE REVERSE FOR HOW TO READ THE SUMMARY REPORT

4th Edition   ©1997, 2001 Rebus Inc.

The Work Sampling System®
©2001 Rebus Inc.

CHILD Brian Dillard

TEACHER Tracy Johnson

SCHOOL

ATTENDANCE: DAYS TARDY _____ DAYS ABSENT 5

AGE/GRADE Fourth Grade

DATE November 1994

The Work Sampling System.
Summary Report

FALL ☑
WINTER ☐
YEAR-END ☐

PERFORMANCE
CHECKLIST   PORTFOLIO   PROGRESS

GENERAL COMMENTS: Give reasons for "Needs Development" and/or note special strengths and talents in each domain. Also give explanation if progress is other than expected. Describe plans for supporting child's growth.

DOMAINS & COMPONENTS

I Personal & Social Development
Self concept
Self control
Approaches to learning
Interaction with others
Social problem-solving

Brian is a highly motivated student who takes a tremendous amount of initiative in his school work. He is enthusiastic about assignments and has a wealth of background knowledge in many areas. Working collaboratively with peers on projects poses a challenge for him. He recognizes his tendency to hold on too firmly to his opinions and we are working together to help him be more open to the ideas of others as well to express his ideas in ways that help his classmates to listen to him. His work tends to be disorganized, the result of working quickly on assignments. When we review his work together, he sees that it could have been better organized.

II Language & Literacy
Listening
Speaking
Reading
Writing
Research (3-5)

Brian is an active listener and speaker during our group meetings and discussions. He takes in the ideas of others and can express his ideas as a way of trying to sort out information. He is comfortable with explaining his ideas although sometimes he loses his peers as he tries to express his ideas as quickly as he is thinking them! Brian is an avid reader and appreciates a variety of literature. Brian enjoys using his imagination in his writing. He writes of an audience and is interested in maintaining their attention. Like other fourth graders he likes to write out his creative ideas and then consider it finished. A goal for Brian is to focus on organizing and revising his writing.

III Mathematical Thinking
Mathematical processes
Number and operations
Patterns, relationships, & functions
Geometry and spatial relations
Measurement
Data collection and probability (K-5)

Mathematical thinking is an area of strength for Brian. He is quick to identify a strategy to solve challenging problems and is systematic in applying it. He has a firm understanding of addition, subtraction, and multiplication. I am working with him to describe clearly both orally and in writing his process of solving problems.

IV Scientific Thinking
Inquiry
Physical science (K-5)
Life science (K-5)
Earth science (K-5)

Brian has a great deal of prior knowledge and experience which he applies to scientific investigations. His research about the Biosphere II reveals clear understanding. He can easily describe how animals adapt to their environment and the food chain, two concepts we have worked on this fall.

V Social Studies
People, past and present
Human interdependence
Citizenship and government
People and where they live

Brian shows some understanding of how human needs have impacted on the environment. Throughout our study of pollution, he continually made comparisons between local pollution issues and situations in other parts of the world.

VI The Arts
Expression and representation
Understanding and appreciation

Brian enjoys projects that involve the visual arts. In this area, he takes the time to plan and complete projects so that he feels a sense of personal pride in the product. He also likes to sing and is involved with the school chorus. He is studying clarinet for the first time this year.

VII Physical Development & Health
Gross motor development
Fine motor development
Personal health and safety

Brian demonstrates coordination and control when using classroom materials. He loves outdoor sports and is a skilled player.

SEE REVERSE FOR HOW TO READ THE SUMMARY REPORT

WHITE – FAMILY   YELLOW – OFFICE   PINK – TEACHER

4th Edition   ©1997, 2001 Rebus Inc

The Work Sampling System®
©2001 Rebus Inc.

The Work Sampling System.
Summary Report

FALL ☐
WINTER ☑
YEAR-END ☐

CHILD Serena Porter
TEACHER Mr. Groves
SCHOOL George Washington Elementary School
AGE/GRADE Third Grade
DATE 2/29/96

ATTENDANCE: DAYS TARDY 0   DAYS ABSENT 1

DOMAINS & COMPONENTS

I Personal & Social Development
Self concept
Self control
Approaches to learning
Interaction with others
Social problem-solving

II Language & Literacy
Listening
Speaking
Reading
Writing
Research (3-5)

III Mathematical Thinking
Mathematical processes
Number and operations
Patterns, relationships, and functions
Geometry and spatial relations
Measurement
Data collection and probability (K-5)

IV Scientific Thinking
Inquiry
Physical science (K-5)
Life science (K-5)
Earth science (K-5)

V Social Studies
People past and present
Human interdependence
Citizenship and government
People and where they live

VI The Arts
Expression and representation
Understanding and appreciation

VII Physical Development & Health
Gross motor development
Fine motor development
Personal health and safety

PERFORMANCE — CHECKLIST / PORTFOLIO
As Expected / Needs Development
PROGRESS — As Expected / Other than Expected

GENERAL COMMENTS: Give reasons for "Needs Development" and/or note special strengths and talents in each domain. Also give explanation if progress is other than expected. Describe plans for supporting child's growth.

Serena gets along well with her classmates and teachers. She works out conflicts in appropriate ways. She is confident in her ability and participates in class discussions. Serena still has problems with organizational skills -- she needs reminders to get started, to stay on task, to complete her assignments. The interventions I've tried so far have not helped. My goal during the next few months will be to go over her work with her daily and give her time after school to complete her assignments. Her portfolio reflects her good thinking, but also shows her difficulty in completing tasks.

Serena continues to progress in her ability to read grade level texts independently and with comprehension. She has special ability in her writing. Not only does she use conventionally spelled words, she also uses capitalization and punctuation correctly. Her stories are well organized and filled with humor.

Serena has good problem solving strategies. She can mentally and quickly work out solutions to problems involving addition, subtraction, multiplication and division. She was able to quickly grasp the concept of using parentheses in problems to change the answer. My goal for her during the next few months is for her to complete math assignments that require several steps and to record her thinking in writing when solving mathematical problems.

Serena uses scientific thinking skills when conducting scientific investigations and research projects. Serena compiled a list of facts she learned about fish during our river study. She did these from memory and stated that fish need water to get oxygen. Her description of how a river starts included parts of the water cycle and the fact that the treatment plant adds chlorine and fluoride to the water.

Serena is a keen observer and remembers many details from our trips. She wrote a lengthy detailed piece about our trip to the water treatment plant. She remembered and wrote about many of the jobs and equipment we saw there. She again mentioned that chemicals were added to the water to clean it. She is able to show through discussion, writing and drawing the differences between the present and the past.

She uses her ability to draw and paint to share knowledge. An example of this is her picture of clothing and transportation used in Pittsburgh long ago. She performed a dance with precision and enthusiasm for our African American history program. She also perfored songs with the class.

Her fine and gross motor skills are highly developed as evidenced by her small precise writing, her building of trees and bushes for our river model and her agility during physical education classes.

SEE REVERSE FOR HOW TO READ THE SUMMARY REPORT   4th Edition   ©1997 2001 Rebus Inc.

WHITE – FAMILY   YELLOW – OFFICE   PINK – TEACHER

The Work Sampling System®
©2001 Rebus Inc.

CHILD _____ Robert Stevens

TEACHER _____ Alice Miller

SCHOOL _____

ATTENDANCE: DAYS TARDY _____   DAYS ABSENT _____ 3

AGE/GRADE _____ ThirdGrade

DATE _____ November 1993

The Work Sampling System.
Summary Report

FALL ☑
WINTER ☐
YEAR-END ☐

PROGRESS

GENERAL COMMENTS: Give reasons for "Needs Development" and/or note special strengths and talents in each domain. Also give explanation if progress is other than expected. Describe plans for supporting child's growth.

I Personal & Social Development
Self concept
Self control
Approaches to learning
Interaction with others
Social problem-solving

Robert is well liked by his peers and very helpful in class. He interacts with his teachers and peers more easily now than at the beginning of the year. I would like to see Robert show more initiative and self-direction when doing and following through on projects. We have been working on this by making detailed work plans that include time expectations. Robert has been taking a few minutes after each work period to review his plan and reflect on his accomplishments. I am encouraging him to invest more ownership in his work.

II Language & Literacy
Listening
Speaking
Reading
Writing
Research (3-5)

Robert has shown improvement in reading since September. I'm certain that his nightly reading at home has helped. He uses several different strategies to understand text. Language — both expressive and receptive — poses a challenge for him. He has difficulty listening and understanding directions and it is hard for him to convey ideas in discussions and conversations. I encourage him to use other methods, especially drawing, to express his ideas and knowledge. Opportunities to talk and listen in groups of only two or three are helping Robert to improve his language skills.

III Mathematical Thinking
Mathematical processes
Number and operations
Patterns, relationships, and functions
Geometry and spatial relations
Measurement
Data collection and probability (3-5)

Robert enjoys math and will work on tasks independently and with persistence. He uses strategies to add and subtract two and three digit numbers and understands regrouping. Reading and writing word problems are difficult for him; he benefits from working with a partner on these tasks. Robert has grasped the concept of graphing and especially enjoys the artistic aspect of this work. Similarly, his work on patterns and spatial relationships is very strong. I will continue to provide Robert with problems that challenge his fine spatial thinking skills.

IV Scientific Thinking
Inquiry
Physical science (K-5)
Life science (K-5)
Earth science (K-5)

Robert worked hard on our ocean unit. He was involved in observations and making new discoveries. Once again, his artistic talents served him well both in drawing observations and creating models. We have begun working on a study of the outdoor environment of our school. He enthusiastically explores his outdoor site and shows initiative in posing questions and thinking through experiments.

V Social Studies
People, past and present
Human interdependence
Citizenship and government
People and where they live

Robert demonstrated good thinking skills in our study of the Wampanaag Indians. As in science, he posed many interesting questions and applied previously learned information to new situations. Robert expresses what he knows in Social Studies using drawing, model making, and dramatization. He is able to read and make simple maps.

VI The Arts
Expression and representation
Understanding and appreciation

Robert is a very artistic child who enjoys making things. His knowledge in other academic areas is best expressed through the arts. For example, he designed detailed graphs in math and consistently made intricate drawings of science observations. He also likes to draw cartoons. His favorite part of writing stories is illustrating them.

VII Physical Development & Health
Gross motor development
Fine motor development
Personal health and safety

Robert has excellent fine motor skills, as demonstrated through his model making and drawing. He hesitates to take part in outdoor play activities because it is difficult for him to perform the gross motor skills needed. He needs practice throwing, catching, and kicking a ball.

PERFORMANCE

CHECKLIST — As Expected / Needs Development

PORTFOLIO — As Expected / Needs Development

PROGRESS — As Expected / Other than Expected

DOMAINS & COMPONENTS

SEE REVERSE FOR HOW TO READ THE SUMMARY REPORT

WHITE – FAMILY   YELLOW – OFFICE   PINK – TEACHER

4th Edition   ©1997, 2001 Rebus Inc

The Work Sampling System®
©2001 Rebus Inc.

The Work Sampling System®
Summary Report

CHILD _Raashan Jackson_   AGE/GRADE _Fifth Grade_

TEACHER _Paulina Richardson_   DATE _November 1994_

SCHOOL _____

ATTENDANCE: DAYS TARDY _____   DAYS ABSENT __1__

FALL ☑
WINTER ☐
YEAR-END ☐

GENERAL COMMENTS: Give reasons for "Needs Development" and/or note special strengths and talents in each domain. Also give explanation if progress is other than expected. Describe plans for supporting child's growth.

DOMAINS & COMPONENTS

I Personal & Social Development
Self concept
Self control
Approaches to learning
Interaction with others
Social problem-solving

Raashan is a responsible student who works well independently and in cooperative projects. He is a gifted mediator, using discussion and compromise to resolve conflicts. I have been encouraging him to set personal goals for his work and to reflect on how he is doing as he works on tasks.

II Language & Literacy
Listening
Speaking
Reading
Writing

In group discussions Raashan is an active participant. He expresses his own ideas coherently and responds to others' ideas. He is a fluent and enthusiastic reader, seeking out specific authors and topics of personal interest. He is quick to offer book suggestions to his peers. Raashan expresses himself easily in writing and has begun to use punctuation and syntax with some accuracy. My writing conferences with Raashan have focused on improving organization of his writing. He needs to think through his ideas before he begins to write.

III Mathematical Thinking
Mathematical processes
Number and operations
Patterns, relationships, and functions
Geometry and spatial relations
Measurement
Data collection and probability (3-5)

Raashan has begun to use appropriate strategies for solving multiplication and division and he can explain his thinking. He is a resourceful thinker, quickly noting patterns, using estimation, and mental arithmetic to help him figure out solutions to problems.

IV Scientific Thinking
Inquiry
Physical science (K-5)
Life science (K-5)
Earth science (K-5)

Raashan took a strong interest in our study of the Savannah grasslands. His project on animals of the night reflected careful research and thinking. During our discussions of the food chain, he used information gained from photographs, videos, and books to formulate questions and make predictions.

V Social Studies
People, past and present
Human interdependence
Citizenship and government
People and where they live

We have just begun our study of the Masai people. In discussion Raashan draws on our study of the Savannah and what he previously learned about the Inuit to consider how the Masai live. He is extremely interested in the myths and folk tales we've been reading about the Masai.

VI The Arts
Expression and representation
Understanding and appreciation

Raashan has taken an interest in painting this year, particularly as a way to convey what he is learning about Africa. He also enjoys dramatics, frequently using dramatization as a way to respond to class literature assignments.

VII Physical Development & Health
Gross motor development
Fine motor development
Personal health and safety

Sports are a special interest for him. His strength as a mediator and his ease with his peers allow him not only to excel at the skill aspect of sports but also at making the games proceed effectively.

SEE REVERSE FOR HOW TO READ THE SUMMARY REPORT   4th Edition   © 1997, 2001 Rebus Inc.

WHITE – FAMILY   YELLOW – OFFICE   PINK – TEACHER

The Work Sampling System®
©2001 Rebus Inc.